$\mathcal{M}$etamorphecise

The Transformation Within

"Exercise your mind, body, and spirit"

Lisa Dwoskin

BALBOA.
PRESS

A DIVISION OF HAY HOUSE

Copyright © 2014 Lisa Dwoskin.

Photography by: Ginelle Lago
http://www.gmnartistic.com/

All rights reserved. No part of this book may be used or reproduced by
any means, graphic, electronic, or mechanical, including photocopying,
recording, taping or by any information storage retrieval system
without the written permission of the publisher except in the case
of brief quotations embodied in critical articles and reviews.

Balboa Press books may be ordered through booksellers or by contacting:

Balboa Press
A Division of Hay House
1663 Liberty Drive
Bloomington, IN 47403
www.balboapress.com
1 (877) 407-4847

Because of the dynamic nature of the Internet, any web addresses or
links contained in this book may have changed since publication and
may no longer be valid. The views expressed in this work are solely those
of the author and do not necessarily reflect the views of the publisher,
and the publisher hereby disclaims any responsibility for them.

The author of this book does not dispense medical advice or prescribe the use
of any technique as a form of treatment for physical, emotional, or medical
problems without the advice of a physician, either directly or indirectly. The
intent of the author is only to offer information of a general nature to help
you in your quest for emotional and spiritual well-being. In the event you use
any of the information in this book for yourself, which is your constitutional
right, the author and the publisher assume no responsibility for your actions.

Any people depicted in stock imagery provided by Thinkstock are
models, and such images are being used for illustrative purposes only.
Certain stock imagery © Thinkstock.

Printed in the United States of America.

ISBN: 978-1-4525-1914-2 (sc)
ISBN: 978-1-4525-1915-9 (e)

Library of Congress Control Number: 2014913094

Balboa Press rev. date: 08/05/2014

Dear Jorge,

This book is dedicated to you. When you died, I was devastated, sad, lost, confused, and heartbroken. I felt at that moment that my life was over. I had finally found my soul mate, and then you left me. We had our whole lives ahead to share and enjoy together, and I was too young to have lost you.

What was later shown to me was that you would forever be my guardian angel and you would guide me and direct me toward my life's destiny. The signs and quotes that we shared when you were alive, you now use to let me know you are opening doors and helping me every step of the way. When I hurt, cry, or feel alone, you always give me a sign to let me know you are at my side. You've made me believe and become open to living a spiritually enlightened life.

Thank you for your eternal love and guidance. I will never forget you.

—Lisa

$\mathcal{C}$ontents

$\mathcal{P}$reface

Metamorphecise is about the transformation within, the journey from the caterpillar to a butterfly. This book is a memoir of my personal journey of becoming spiritually enlightened and emerging into my true self. In it, I discuss the many challenges and losses that I have faced and worked through along the way, challenges that helped me grow into a better person. Life is filled with trials and tribulations; how we handle these challenges molds us into the people that we will become.

In the book, I also teach my readers how to help themselves and learn to become healthier and happier. I have learned that there is work that needs to be done. In the same way that we work on our bodies with exercise and good nutrition, we must work on exercising our minds and spirits. I include daily rituals and homework that enable us to break free from old patterns. I teach others to break the patterns, change their thoughts, feed their mind with positivity and self-love, and set themselves free. My readers will learn to stop the mind chatter, clutter, and negative self-talk, stay away from people who drain their energy, and instead surround themselves with positive people that feed their soul and lift them up.

I have been a fitness instructor, spa and wellness center owner, and life coach most of my life, and I love to teach and educate people on how to live happy and fulfilled lives. What I have learned about myself throughout the last several years is that exercising the body is not enough; one must exercise the mind and spirit as well to become whole. I used to escape to exercise to find peace and forget about challenges in my life. What I wasn't doing was silencing my mind and listening to my spirit to guide me.

This book tells my own personal story and explains the different stages of life that I had to go through to help me understand what my soul was trying to teach me. I needed to let go of many things from the past, stop worrying about the future, and just live in the moment. I needed to love myself more and stop trying to help others before myself. I needed to just *be* in the moment every second, every minute, every day. With the faith that I have always had in God, my higher source, and the universe, I needed to continue to move forward through challenges and losses, knowing that all will be okay. I was enough!

Meditation is a major component of my own personal growth and of my method for encouraging people to grow and become more spiritually enlightened. In the book and in my seminars, I teach that meditation should be done on a daily basis, between ten and sixty minutes at a time. It will be difficult at first, but it will become easier with practice, and I encourage my readers to keep practicing. When a person learns to silence their mind, the truth will reveal itself and you will know what your soul needs to become. Too many people live while tying their souls down. "Free your mind, and free your spirit" is my message.

I guide and teach how to live from a state of gratitude, love, joy, peace, and happiness. I believe that everyone deserves to live a life filled with abundance; the universe wants this for all of us. I am so happy to share a message of "Believe, and you will achieve greatness" and help my readers find out how simple it is to live a life filled with happiness. This book will offer simple and easy steps to strengthen my reader's spiritually driven life and teach them to live from a more soul-centered place.

As a fitness professional and life coach in my daily life, I teach people how to exercise, eat healthy, feed their minds with positivity, and learn how to become healthier and happier. I teach people to want to learn and grow and live a life of longevity, here and now. My message both in person and in my book is that people do not need to wait for their lives to be better to become happier; they need to live now. I encourage people not to wait for the perfect job, perfect weight, or perfect mate but to be happy within, and all the others will come. Self-love and inner happiness are what you need to live a fulfilled life.

We all want to become healthier and happier, but who wants to learn and put the effort into your workouts to achieve the happiness? I am here to encourage my readers to do just that! These workouts include exercising the mind, body, and spirit, and they truly do work. It takes effort, but nothing in life comes easy. We must challenge ourselves to grow and emerge to a better state.

Great teachers have helped, guided, and blessed me throughout my own journey. I met amazing people along the way that didn't even know they were guiding me to greater spiritual teachings. This is what I want *Metamorphecise* to do for my readers. I want to guide, teach, motivate, and inspire. We all want to emerge into the beautiful butterfly, expand our wings, and fly. Let me help guide you to become that butterfly.

Metamorphecise is the journey of becoming the beautiful butterfly that you were meant to be. We all start out as that little caterpillar squirming along through life. When and where we transform our minds, bodies, and spirits is where we can transform our lives and become the beautiful butterfly. *Metamorphecise* is the transformation within that a person must experience to emerge to the true self, the true *you*.

Come and experience this journey with me. Read and enjoy my experiences, and learn how I transformed. It is so simple to learn, grow, and be happy. I am so excited to share my *Metamorphecise* with others to teach them that they can do it too.

Chapter 1

The Beginning

I knew when I was eighteen years old that I wanted to open a gym one day, because I loved fitness. My late boyfriend, Jorge, was a major influence.

When I was eighteen, my boyfriend at that time played baseball with my father and brother. Watching them play was where I saw Jorge for the first time. Jorge's looks and athletic ability took my breath away. He had a wife and son that came to the games, and although I had a boyfriend, I enjoyed watching Jorge play. I found out that he owned and operated a gym, which I thought was so cool. I had been with my boyfriend since I was fifteen. We had a great relationship that continued until I was twenty-three and went away to college, then we drifted apart.

I transferred from three different colleges until I ended up back in Florida, my home state, and graduated from the University of Miami with a degree in psychology and a minor in exercise physiology. During my time at the University of Florida, my major was exercise science, where I studied the human body. Although I enjoyed this very much, I also found psychology very intriguing because I loved to study the human mind. I have the gift of listening to and advising people to help them heal, so I decided to switch my major because I wanted to learn more about the mind-body connection. Knowing that at a very young age I wanted to open a wellness center one day, my dad gave me an assignment: to learn and get as much experience as I could before he would help me open my very own center.

My father, who was a very successful businessman, knew exactly what it took to open my own business. He told me I needed to start from the bottom and learn every aspect and detail possible before I would be ready to open my own center. He gave me a timeline of ten years to learn what I needed to before he would financially help me. I knew he was right because he had done it himself.

When I was twenty-two, I graduated from college and decided to work for my dad's business and teach fitness on the side. However, my dad and I did not see eye to eye when it came to his business. My heart was not into auto parts; it was into health and wellness. I also did not want to be under my dad's wing and needed to branch out on my own where my passion lay. This was when I took the leap and went into fitness full time.

I drove down to South Beach one day to try to locate an old friend who had opened a gym. I had no idea what the name was, but when I stopped to get a protein shake, I saw a guy with a T-shirt from a local gym. It happened to be my friend's. This is how every aspect of my life played out. I would send out a request, and the universe would respond, just like that.

I was so happy to have found the gym. My friend gave me a job, and that started my new path in the fitness business. I later ended up leasing his gym for a year to learn more and be ready to open my own in the future.

I lived in South Beach for seven years. During this time, I ran into Jorge everywhere. I bumped into him in restaurants, movie theaters, and even elevators, until one night, we met at a dance club. The stars were aligned because he had just gotten divorced and I had broken up with my boyfriend. We started dating and had an on-again, off-again relationship for about three years. It was not a healthy relationship. It was more like an addiction, a certain connection that is indescribable. We did have great communication and great times when we were together though. We shared our dreams, goals, and desires and could talk for hours. We laughed a lot and had so much fun together. It was just that we would break up every three months or so, which was pure heartache.

Jorge taught me about spiritual signs and connections. He had lost his mother to breast cancer when he was twenty-eight years old. He taught me about the number 11:11, which he felt was a sign from her. Also, he would find pennies everywhere and tell me it was her way of connecting with him. I loved hearing this because I have always been a big believer in life after death and that our loved ones are always with us even after they pass on.

My great grandmother was clairvoyant. She would see things happen before they actually did. My mother is also very much in touch with her spiritual side. She has had visits from her father after he passed. One night, when she was going through a very difficult time, she woke up and saw her father sitting at the side of her bed. He told her that everything would be okay. She knew this was a visit because she was wide-awake.

I experienced the same thing one night while on a ski trip with Jorge and my family. Jorge's mother appeared to me in a dream and told me how happy she was that I was in his life. We talked for a while, and I remembered it as if it had really happened. I had never met her, but I described to Jorge what she looked like in detail. He was so happy. I had never seen a picture of her before the dream, and it was definitely her. Even more amazing about this experience was that I dreamed of her on January 5, the night I was due to be born. My mom told me that they had induced me because of complications, which was why I was born in December. Jorge was so shocked and told me that January 5 was the anniversary of his mother's death. The day I was supposed to be born, the day she died, and the night I had the dream all were January 5. I knew this was a definite connection, but I had no idea how strong the connections would become in the near future.

Jorge died suddenly in 1999. I was twenty-eight years old, the age he was when his mother had died. He died at thirty-four years old from an inexplicable reason for which we will never have answers. The day he died, I was doing a breast cancer walk with my very close friend. I remember saying a minute before the race began that I should get a sign, write the name of Jorge's mom on my chest, and dedicate the walk to her. At that exact moment, the loudest gunshot went off, signaling that the race had begun. Startled, we began to walk. Little did I know that Jorge had just died from a gunshot wound to his chest. It was as if his mom were sending me a signal.

Immediately after the race, I found out about Jorge, and my life turned upside down.

The healing process was extremely difficult, because there was no explanation as to what had happened, just many theories and hearsay. I was in shock and pain and filled with questions.

During this time, I was in the middle of my lease with the gym in South Beach and still perfecting my trade. I was reaching the ten-year timeline my dad had given me and was nearly ready to open my own wellness center. One day while at the gym, a member gave me a CD called *Metamorphosis*. He told me to listen to it, try to relax, and it would help heal my heartbreak.

This CD was the only thing that brought temporary peace to my mind and soul. The more I meditated, the more I felt I was transforming from caterpillar to butterfly. Metamorphosis was slowly occurring in me as my mind, body, and spirit transformed.

I finished the one-year lease with the gym and began looking for my own location. As I was teaching a spin class one day at a local gym, I stumbled upon a notice about a location the owner was going to purchase but was backing out of. I jumped in my car and found the new site was zoned for a gym. It was much larger than I wanted, but I could see my dream of my very own wellness center in that exact location. The community required a spa and health club, and it was very strict with the size and specs. It was the total package. My father was very concerned about the size of the building and the amount of work and responsibility I was setting myself up for. I agreed with him, but he knew that when my mind was set on something, I fought till the end. I had a calling that was too strong to ignore.

After one year of negotiating with the landlord, we finalized the deal.

During that year, the meditation CD really helped me heal from Jorge's death, but it was a long and difficult process. I believed that if it could help me, it could also help many others, so I decided to use it in my new wellness center. I named the wellness center Metamorphecise, which means, "The transformation begins within."

Two very close friends helped me design the logo. It came to life one night when the three of us, after drinking some wine, started doing yoga poses and acting silly. We had so much fun and the logo was designed while my friend and I did the pose and my other friend drew it on her computer. I had the name, logo, and location all set. Now the concept was ready to launch as a wellness center to transform people's lives through exercise and healthy thinking and living.

Chapter 2

Follow the Signs

After negotiating for one year, my father, my landlord, and I finally came to an agreement and the papers were signed. The day we signed the contract was January 5, 2001. I had nothing to do with the date; it was all about organizing a time between two very busy men to get together and help me put this deal into place. When I realized that the day was January 5, I knew without a shadow of doubt that Jorge and his mother were telling me that this was meant to be. Remember this was the day I was supposed to be born, the day Jorge's mother died, and the day I had the dream of her—not a coincidence at all.

The address of the building was another powerful sign from Jorge: 111 Grand Palms Drive. Wow! This was the number that Jorge and I talked about all the time: 1:11 and 11:11. I also used to tell Jorge that, whether we were together or apart, one day he would walk into my gym and tell me how proud he was of me for accomplishing my goals and reaching my dreams. We also talked about butterflies a lot and how he would come to me as a purple butterfly because that was my favorite color. He used to talk as if he knew he was going to die young, but I would tell him to stop because it made me sad.

For a couple of months, I did a presale of memberships and started to design the layout of the building. It was a large building—17,000 square feet to be exact. I was told by my landlord, to design a spa, salon, and health club. I had never designed anything but wanted to do it myself, without hiring an expert to do it for me. I did have people advise me, but in the end, I design everything myself. It was as if a force greater than me was guiding me every step of the way. Every detail—plants, paintings, murals, waterfalls, décor— came together perfectly. I had become a spa, salon, gym, and design expert, all within a couple of months.

One afternoon, while I was meeting with the general contractor about the build-out, an extraordinary thing happened. The extremely heavy door flew open very loudly and a lavender butterfly came floating in. I was overcome with emotion. I knew it was Jorge, because this is how he did everything—larger than life. Instead of crying or being scared, I just smiled and felt peace in my heart and soul.

During the presale and setup of the business, I began dating a very close friend who had helped me get through the loss of Jorge. I met Matt six months after Jorge died, and he helped me through a very difficult time in my life. He was patient and understanding of what I was going through and never pressured me to move on right away. He had been a marine and firefighter, and a very active bodybuilder, so it was a perfect match. We had a lot in common and had fun together. I asked him if he wanted to work with me, and since his lawn business was boring him and he enjoyed fitness, he agreed. He put 100 percent effort into helping me with the entire start-up of the business. His strengths were my weaknesses, and vice versa. I enjoyed that I could be myself with him, and we both loved being with one another. As time went on, we grew closer and fell in love. We married two years later.

Metamorphecise was up and running a year before we got married, and people loved it. Members loved the fact that they could exercise and pamper themselves all in one place. We also had seminars for healing, meditation and hypnotherapy classes, astrology readings, wine and cheese parties, and a full-service juice bar. It was a place to transform your being and escape the mundane of your everyday life.

Over the next five years, we built a wonderful family within the business, both employees and members. We helped so many people go through many difficult moments in their lives: deaths of loved ones, cancers, divorce, etc. I was overcome with joy that we could help so many people to transform their mind, body, and spirit.

Matt and I also started our own family. We had a daughter first and then a son. We were very happy, but we also worked very hard—about sixty hours a week—so we raised our kids within our business. We built a daycare with cribs within the center and hired a nanny to help us with the kids. The first three or four years it was fun and easy, but as they got older, we had to make adjustments to make sure the kids were getting enough time with us as well. When you are running a business of this magnitude and balancing a family, it is not an easy task. This put a bit of a strain on our marriage as well.

Things were going pretty well until the economy took a turn in late 2008. This became a very stressful time for Matt and me. Our business was very much affected, our marriage was becoming very difficult, and my health was taking a beating.

I had been feeling very weak and off balance for about eight years, and it seemed to be getting worse. I also started to get long spurts of severe vertigo, where everything would be spinning and I felt like I had a brain tumor. Vertigo is very scary if you have ever experienced it, especially when it would not go away for months at a time. I remember training clients many times and feeling like the floor was falling down beneath my feet, kind of like a ride where the ground falls down. I had been seeing so many flashes of light in my vision for so many years, I just assumed that it was Jorge or little angels appearing to me. It looked like what you see after someone takes a picture with a flash. I went to many specialists and doctors trying to figure out why I had these symptoms, or why the vertigo would not go away, but no one could give me answers. The doctors would say it was stress from my life or symptoms from my pregnancy hormones. About two to three times a month, I also experienced migraines so severe that they would cause me to vomit for hours each time.

I remember one time I was in a meeting with a gentleman about a martial arts school. As he was talking, I started to see those flashes of light, and they went from about five to five hundred to five thousand. There were so many flashes that his entire face became distorted, and so did the entire room. I later learned that when this happened, I would have to immediately get to a dark room and put ice on my head or I would get a severe migraine and vomiting. Sometimes, it would go away and other times I would suffer for four to six hours and nothing helped.

I managed to live with all these symptoms until one day it got worse. That day, I was getting ready to teach my spin class. Suddenly, I had that feeling of the ground dropping and a loss of balance, and then I could not see out of my right eye at all for about five minutes. I held on to the wall without anyone noticing and waited until I was back to normal. I called Matt to come upstairs and quietly told him to check on me throughout the class in case I passed out and call 911 if needed. I think by this point, he was so used to all my symptoms that he thought I was a little cuckoo. Needless to say, I made it through the class and felt fine afterward. That night I called my mom and told her about it and she was so upset with me for teaching and told me I must see a heart doctor. She had been watching Dr. Oz the day before and he was talking about all the symptoms that I was sharing being a heart condition.

My mom, being the greatest mom in the world, got on a plane the next day from Seattle to Florida to make sure I went to the doctor. My father had a foundation at the University of Miami, and that is where we would go for all medical problems. We went to the top heart surgeon at the hospital, and although he had a long waiting list, my dad got me in the next day. Dr. William O'Neil examined me and just sat and talked to me for ten minutes. After hearing my symptoms, he immediately diagnosed me with a PFO, a hole in my heart, and ordered me to have tests the following day.

We are all born with a hole in our heart and at about age one or two it closes up. Some do not fully close and can live like that; about 2 percent need to have the hole fixed because it stops the oxygen from flowing from the heart to the brain. If it is not fixed, the lack of oxygen will cause mini strokes and probably a major stroke, or death.

First, I had an ultrasound and they did find a hole, but they needed another test to see how large the hole was. The second test took thirty minutes for the practitioner to set up. First, they put a crown around my head that looked like Christ's crown of thorns. Then they placed an IV in my arm to put saline in, and at the same time, I had to push as hard as I could with my stomach. I had to take a deep breath and push my stomach out as hard as I could; this measured the amount of oxygen being carried from my heart to my brain. If any bubbles showed up on the computer, then it meant I was lacking oxygen in certain areas.

When the results came in, the entire screen was filled with bubbles. I remember looking at my mom and tears were rolling down my face because I was overwhelmed with the fear of dying. I went downstairs to wait to see the doctor and called my dad to tell him. I remember hearing such fear in my dad's voice because he could usually control all aspects of his life, but not this. He was strong and went right to work figuring out what we would do next, but I knew that he was overcome with fear.

Dr. O'Neill decided to do the surgery the following week to close up the hole. They had found that I had had numerous mini strokes over the years and did not want it to get worse. All those times that I had the flashes of light and felt the floor drop beneath my feet around—those were all mini strokes.

The morning of the surgery, when they were prepping me in the operating room, another very spiritual event took place. I had painted my toenails blue and my finger nails purple because those are two of my favorite colors. I had read a lot about the archangel Michael and how he is the angel that protects and heals. You will know that he is in your presence if you start to see a lot of purple and blue because those colors are his symbolic colors. There was a very sweet male nurse prepping me right before they put me to sleep. He was wearing blue scrubs, and a purple bandana was tied around his head. I told him that I loved the bandana because purple was my favorite color. He said, "Funny thing is, I have had this bandana for years and never wore it, and when I woke up this morning, something told me to wear it. I guess it was for you and your surgery." I knew that this was a sign from my spirit guides telling me that everything would be okay—I was protected.

The surgery was a success. The doctor told my parents that the hole was very large and that I could have had a massive stroke, or been in a coma without the surgery. Now, we could all rest, assured that I would be fine.

Two weeks later, I was back to my regular exercise routine. My doctor told me that exercise is what saved my life, because my heart was in such great shape.

Chapter 3

Destiny Will Find You

Although my surgery was a success and my health was much better, my marriage and business were both falling apart. The economy played a big role in the deterioration of my business, but my main focus became my kids, health, and marriage. In the beginning of 2011, I decided to take my mom on a cruise that I had paid for the year before, when I found out that Wayne Dyer would be there. I knew if my husband and I were not doing well, my mom would love to come with me. It was a spiritual, healing cruise, so she and I would have a great time. It was called "You Can Heal Your Life." Back in 2009, my friend had talked to me about Wayne Dyer and felt that his books and knowledge would help me get through difficult times in my life. I bought some of his books and started learning more about intentions and changing one's thinking. I also began to meditate and silence my mind. I became infatuated with all of Wayne Dyer's teaching and read every one of his books.

I felt a great connection with him, and he helped me through many difficult times.

Ironically, the same friend who introduced me to Wayne Dyer's work ended up in a coma and almost died. When a medical team found him in his apartment, he was almost dead from pneumonia and dehydration. He was brought to the hospital in a coma. His friends and I took turns sitting with him, and I decided to stay the night. This friend was like a brother to me and I could not leave his side until his family arrived. Since his family lives in Colombia and had to travel to the hospital, this took a few days. The hospital staff let me stay next to him in intensive care the entire night. They knew that if they asked me to leave, I was not going to, so they let me stay. They would not tell me much, but I knew he was in bad shape. During the night, he would get very agitated and try to spit out the tube that was helping him to breathe. The nurse told me that if he spit the tube out, he would not make it through the night.

Usually, I would be so overwhelmed with the fear of death and losing loved ones that I would just panic, but not this night. Instead, I became like Wonder Woman and had enormous amounts of strength for the two of us. I felt that God chose me to be with him to help save his life. I remember standing over him for hours and talking to him about Wayne Dyer and what he had taught us about letting go and letting God guide us. I told him to relax and to breathe, and to find that gap to meditate and stop trying to control the situation.

There was one incident at about 3:30 a.m. when he got very agitated, trying to spit the tube out. Until this point, I was calm and talking very sweetly for many hours to help him relax, breathe, and heal, and then I became a little abrupt. I very loudly and aggressively told him, "Stop!" I said, "Listen to me, and listen good. I will *not* let you die! *Stop* trying to spit that damn tube out, right now! You must stop! If you continue to do that, you will die! You are not ready to die, and I am not ready to let you go! You must relax and do it now!" Okay, so it wasn't so peaceful and soothing, but it worked, he stopped.

I believed so much that God and the universe made it so that I could be with him at this crucial moment.

My friend had guided me toward Wayne Dyer's teaching and it helped my life, and in turn, I helped save his life. My friend made it through the night and was hospitalized for two months. After many surgeries and struggles, he is completely back to a healthy and happy lifestyle. This showed me that the mind is such a powerful tool, and Wayne Dyer's teachings were drawing me in even more. I could not wait to meet him in person on the cruise.

As my mom and I walked on the cruise ship, we were both so excited to learn more about healing and living with inner peace. Mom had battled breast cancer in 2008, so this was great for both of us. After a quick welcoming drink, we were summoned to get in our designated categories for the lifeboat drills. This ship was *Holland America*, and it was huge, filled with thousands of people traveling to many different destinations.

Out of the thousands of people, guess who was standing right next to me during our lifeboat instructions. Yes, Wayne Dyer! I was so excited to meet him in person, and I know that the universe had a play in this meeting.

He was with a pretty blonde woman, whom I asked to take our picture. I thought she was his wife, but I found out later that she was his nurse practitioner and friend. The next day, we went to his seminar, which lasted nearly three hours. I was enamored by every word and could have sat there for eight hours straight, listening to him. The woman who took our picture also spoke; her name was Pam McDonald. She wrote a book with Hay House called *The Perfect Gene Diet*. This was a book about diet, exercise, and way of living that Wayne Dyer followed to help with his leukemia. I found her research and her work very interesting and wanted to learn more.

Later that day, like every day, I ended up in the gym to do a workout. I had many thoughts of my future on my mind and decided to get on the bike to read a book and ease the stress in my head. I must have looked very stressed out, because the lady on the bike next to me asked, "Are you okay?" I looked over and it was Pam from the seminar. I was so excited to see her and talk to her all about her work, but instead, we ended up talking all about me. I opened up to her about everything that was going on in my life. She has a way of bringing out the inner thoughts of people and exposing their deep-rooted truths. My mom and Pam's friend kept coming over to see how we were, but Pam and I just carried on our conversation for about ninety minutes. My mom later told me that we looked like long-time friends who had known each other for years. I felt like she was my soul sister that I have known from another lifetime. She listened and gave me such great advice as to what to do in my life, and she made such perfect sense. We exchanged numbers and started a lifelong friendship that has had such a huge impact on my journey through life.

The cruise was a magical, magnificent, life-changing trip for both my mom and me. It helped us center our lives and put things into perspective. They taught us about the power of the mind and how it controls the body and soothes the soul. We learned how to live from a more spirit-centered life filled with love and peace and how we must believe, speak, and live in the way that we are meant to be, from the spirit. If we do this and practice this, we will change our lives in such a positive and drastic way.

On one of the cruise days, we went to a private island for outdoor activities. I decided to go horseback riding on the beach where you get to swim with the horses. I thoroughly enjoyed it and met an intriguing woman during the trail ride. She shared with me all the hardships that she had been though in her life and what had led her to come on this cruise. She lived and breathed yoga. That was her escape to healing and centered her life. I needed this talk from her to help get myself into yoga. I had always wanted to, but never was consistent with my practice. She explained how yoga helped change her life and how it would help me relax. I made her and myself a promise that day: I would start yoga as soon as I got back to my gym.

When I came back from the cruise, I started making immediate changes in my life. I began to take yoga classes, and it took a while, but I did enjoy it and learn how to relax. I also found two partners for my business, because I could no longer handle the stress. I took Pam's advice of not selling completely but finding partners to help run the business. My husband started doing other work outside of the business and all seemed to be running smoothly. After months of negotiating the contract, we signed it on April 4.

My partners joined forces with me, and I shared with them all about Pam and what she did with genetic research and how I felt it was a perfect fit to introduce in the wellness centers. I decided to do the APO E gene test with Pam and experience it firsthand before we introduced it into our business. It is fortunate that I did, because I ended up being tested as extremely susceptible to end up with Alzheimer's if I did not tweak a few things in my lifestyle. I had always exercised and eaten healthy foods, but I needed to cut out things that caused my gut to become inflamed.

I loved what Pam was doing and wanted to be part of her business model. My partners and I flew out to California to meet with her and her team and put a business model together. I remember the first dinner we had, things went great and I was super excited. I went to use the restroom with such happiness in my heart, and in the restroom, I heard the song that was the first song Jorge and I danced to. It was one of my favorite songs. I took that as a sign. Funny thing is that the original singer of the song ended up being a member of my gym, and I saw him in concert and became friends. The second sign I got in California was the last night we ate dinner at a restaurant called Jorge's Restaurant, amazingly. That night, we decided that Pam would come down and do a seminar in Florida at our gym. She was extremely busy and had to schedule months out, so she picked the date. She picked 11/11/11, another sign that Jorge was still helping me in guiding my destiny. I was so overcome with excitement and joy and knew that everything was falling in place in my life. The number 1111 is so spiritual and magical. There are many websites that explain the significance of this number and how spiritual it really is for people who are awake and open. The trip was a huge success, and I was so excited for my future with Pam and my partners.

Unfortunately, my marriage once again was troubled. My husband and I could not communicate and we continued to drift apart. It was very sad and stressful to the point where it became unbearable to live together. Once again, we separated around October. The first separation was a month before my heart surgery, and we got back together three months later when his father died.

Toward the beginning of December, I was feeling sad and missed my family being together for the holidays, so I fell into a bit of a slump again. I went to the cemetery where Jorge is buried next to his mother and just sat and prayed for a while. I was talking out loud about how I found two partners and that had helped me tremendously, but that my marriage was still a struggle. I spoke on and on.

As I was speaking, another amazing thing happened. I looked down at the date when his mother had been born, and it was the exact same date when I signed the contract with my partners: April 4. How could it be coincidental that the same day I signed the contract for my business was the day she died, and the day I was relieved with business partners was the day she was born? Especially with all the significance of the January 5 date, everything was connected.

As I sat there, I had chills running up and down my entire body, especially around my neck area where you feel the little tingles of chills. Whenever I speak or hear truth, these chills occur, and then I have an overwhelming sense of peace come across my entire being. I knew at this moment that everything would be okay and was in divine order.

Chapter 4

Giving Is Love

The year 2012 was much easier. My workload was less stressful because of my partners, things with Pam were moving along, and I was excited about my future. I was able to spend more time with my kids, and this was better for them as well as me. Once again, I could not stand the fact of keeping my family apart and asked Matt to please move back in. He felt the same way about our family and agreed.

Since I had become a silent partner, I was able to let go of running the business and focus on what I love to do, which is helping people transform their body, mind, and spirit. I was able to teach spinning and group exercise, and be a life-coach to help people reach their goals. My degree in psychology helped a great deal for me in learning how to get into people's minds and understand what made them tick. I found that when I would guide the individuals with positive affirmations to overcome self-love, self-worth, and self-esteem issues, this would help much more than just body work alone. We also would spend a great deal of time talking about nutrition and how certain people use food as a weapon in their lives. Many would use food to mask their pain, either in excess or deficiency. Everyone has issues and I wanted to help people acknowledge theirs and try to work through them.

Earlier in my career, when I was in my 20s, I would just personal-train my clients and put them through body workouts and then go to my next client or class. I overloaded myself with so much work that I could not give each client the time and dedication that they needed. It is like the doctors who schedule so many patients that they cannot give each one enough of their time. I later realized that I needed to have fewer clients and spend more time getting to know each one's needs. Not only did I keep track of their weight and body fat, I also looked at their nutrition and their inner feelings and emotions. Most of my clients that were obese were suffering from internal pain that they had endured in their lives and did not want to face. I have a way of making people feel comfortable to talk and trust me with their emotions. I feel that God blessed me with a gift of healing, and I need to use it to help people.

In 2005, retired basketball player Shaquille O'Neill had a reality show with six obese kids that needed to get healthy and lose weight. It showed raw footage of their emotional struggles and how and why they gained the weight to begin with. There was always something going on internally. This show touched my heart so much that I knew I had to do more for kids. The show was filmed in Florida, so I reached out to everyone from the show and was able to reach all six kids. Coach Dale Brown was part of the show, and I reached out to him as well.

After an incredible dinner with Dale and my family, he helped me locate everyone from the show and told them that I would be contacting all of them. I guess I made a good impression on Dale as well. I started a childhood obesity prevention group at my gym. All six kids helped me get it started because they were mini celebrities, and the children were so excited to meet them and exercise with them. I gave all six kids jobs, and together we started classes with the coaches from the show as well—two great guys that were also schoolteachers and dedicated their lives to helping kids. The kids were all in their teens and were excited to have paying jobs, while helping kids get in shape.

We implemented a psychological segment to the program, where I would meet with the kids one-on-one every month and lead group discussions about emotional challenges they were facing. At every meeting, someone would share and cry and open his or her heart about struggles with weight and self-esteem. We really made a great impact on these kids' lives. If necessary, I would also meet with the parents and discuss their children's struggles with them. This program lasted about one year and we helped hundreds of kids.

We did not continue it, because I had trouble finding the right people to be involved, and without the original people involved, it kind of fizzled out. I began other kids classes that weren't as thorough, but it still got them exercising and eating healthy. I also got very involved with the coaches in trying to help the school systems implement more PE classes and more nutritious foods. We even went as far as reaching the governor of Florida trying to make movements happen. Shaquille was able to implement better exercise programs in school systems in Florida, and we were very happy about this.

After this program, when I started training clients one-on-one again, I decided to implement the mind, body, and spirit aspects to my program to help people conquer all areas and not just their body issues. I thoroughly enjoyed training people and knew that I truly would help them overcome many challenges in their lives by helping them become aware of what was going on internally as well as externally. I began to realize how the mind controlled all aspects of the body, and without changing the mind, the body will not react accordingly. I started to feed my clients with positive affirmations and gave them homework assignments to train their minds as hard as their bodies on a daily basis. This started my journey as a life coach, and it became the most rewarding job that I could ever ask for. At first, I would become frustrated when clients would not put forth the effort into changing their mind-set, but then I realized that I would help guide them, but only they could make the necessary changes. If they would not change, I felt good in knowing that I tried to help guide them in the right direction. I was not a healer; I was just a teacher in showing how to help themselves heal.

I decided to start implementing the positive affirmation in my group exercise classes. I had thirty to fifty people in these classes, and the reactions were overwhelming. People came to me after class and thanked me for helping them cope with stressors of life. Many told me that I was not only a great instructor but also a great mentor and motivator. Helping people feel happier and giving them hope to believe that they too could become happier made me happy.

I also instructed my students to take three long, deep breaths at the end of class. I told them to breathe in the white light and let out all the darkness, or breathe in all the positive energy and breathe out the negative. They loved this as well because it made them stop and be silent—at least for that moment in time. Sometimes, I picked certain people to say something positive for the day, and it shocked me to see that some individuals could not think of one thing to say. I taught them to say smile, happy, thank-you, peace, love, or joy—any one word would be fine. I never realized how some people had zero positivity in their lives. Wow, this was so hard for me to understand, because I have been such a positive person. Again, this awakened the teacher in me. I needed to help people learn to be more positive in everyday life and become more spiritual.

I truly loved and honored my role as a teacher of healing, and this became my journey to be a life coach of mind, body, and spirit. I would spend hours with clients and non-clients, whether I was getting paid of not. I was so passionate about teaching people to be more positive that it became my life's passion. People truly needed to understand how important it was to feed your mind with positive thoughts and your body with healthy and nutritious foods, and to exercise—all went hand-in-hand. All aspects need to be done on a regular basis as well.

Exercise makes people feel and look better. There are many forms of exercise, and not one particular one is good for everyone. Cardiovascular exercise is essential for everyone to do and comes in many forms: walking, hiking, spinning, biking, running, stepping, or anything that gets your heart pumping faster. The average person should exercise three to five times a week for at least thirty minutes per day. Weight training is also very important for bones and joints, especially when you get older, to prevent osteoporosis. Weights also aid in weight loss and helping your posture. I have had so many people approach me over the years asking how to stay so fit, and the answer is always the same: cardio, weight lifting or resistance training, and healthy eating. So many women would say to me, "I do not want to lift weights because I do not want to get bigger or look like a man" or "I want to lose fat then lift." I would answer, "Do I look like a man?" I actually lift more than lots of men, but I still look feminine. Unless a woman is taking drugs, she cannot look like a man with weight training. Also, women who lose weight without using resistance training lose the muscle as well and become flabby or have loose skin. Muscle mass helps burn more fat and get toned. A solid combination of cardio, weights or resistance training, clean eating, and positive mind-set will improve your life tremendously.

Everyone wants to look and feel better and live longer. This takes effort. Exercise is such a great stress reliever. While you are exercising, the endorphins are released in your brain and automatically make you feel better. Who does not want to feel better? I never could understand how certain people could live without exercise. Don't they understand how great it is for you? I view exercise as I view brushing my teeth: it is a must that I do daily. Some days, I love it, and other days, I don't. But I still do it. Exercise, to me, is *me* time. I let go of all negative thoughts and stress and just go. I feel so free and so empowered when I work out. I feel strong and confident and sexy and beautiful. To me, exercise is heavenly bliss; it is my drug of choice. Others choose alcohol, illegal drugs, or prescription drugs to feel better. I found that exercising can help heal your life. I am so blessed to help teach others how it could help them heal as well.

Chapter 5

Let the Past Stay in the Past

In junior high, I was what you call an ugly duckling. I had big, brown, mousy hair, braces, huge eyes, and freckles. I started to get bullied and teased at age ten, and it lasted till about age fifteen. During those five years, I had kids barking at me, calling me fish eyes, laughing, and harassing me all of the time; it was devastating. Luckily, I had two great parents that loved and supported me and gave me a sense of self. My father, one of the most influential people in my life, was very present in my childhood. He was very driven, determined, positive, and a great role model. As a little girl, my dad was the apple of my eye. He would tell me that I was the smartest and prettiest girl alive. He told me to believe in myself and know that I am great, and not to listen to what others felt about me. He was there for me every day of my life, reassuring me and giving me positive feedback and affirmations. My mother was also very positive, loving, and supportive.

I was blessed with great parents and a great brother. I had the kind of childhood like *The Brady Bunch* family on TV—a lot of wonderful family memories with trips, gatherings, dinners. It was the kind of a childhood that kids dream of having. We had all the kids at our house for parties and boat rides and loads of fun. I grew up with the philosophy of seeing the glass half-full, never half-empty.

By age fifteen, I got my braces off, started wearing makeup, and felt a little prettier. I decided to become a cheerleader, and this started my new attitude about myself. I had my first boyfriend at age sixteen, and he helped me feel better about myself as well. Although I felt better than before, the scars were very deep and hurtful and I carried them with me into my early adulthood. I started teaching fitness at the age of about seventeen, and this made me feel like a different person. I loved to exercise and to help others too. I started teaching classes in college, had a huge following, and made some money doing it. I still had self-esteem issues regarding my outer beauty, but my inner self and my personality overshadowed what I had been through and how I felt about it.

I was such a driven person like my dad, and nothing got in my way of moving forward. I started working for my dad at age seven, answering his WATS lines at his company, sitting with him, and watching everything he did. When all my friends were off to camp, I wanted to work with my dad. In my early teens, my mom had to really take hold of me and teach me how to act like a girl, because I just wanted to mirror everything about my dad. I was not shy about anything. I had common sense and knew how to manipulate to get what I wanted. My parents instilled good core values and principles in me, and my dad instilled the solid hard work ethic. Although my dad became very successful and we had a very good life, he always taught my brother and me the value of a dollar.

As I grew more interested in the fitness business, because of my passion and the fact that Jorge owned a gym, I wanted to own a gym also. My body began to transform and get very fit, and this made me feel much better about my outer appearance. I was with my first boyfriend from age sixteen to age twenty three, and once we broke up, I had no problem meeting men. I was five foot, ten, very fit, and a lot of fun. I felt much prettier and sexier about myself, but still I battled those inner demons from childhood. When my friends and I went out to clubs, I drank a lot to quiet the insecurities in my mind. I had gorgeous friends and we would get into any club in South Beach, back in the day when South Beach was the hottest place to be.

The funny thing is that it was always me getting us all the connections into the clubs. I became known as Lisa Marie, the queen of South Beach; everyone knew me, and we got in anywhere with free drinks all night. What a life. I had bleached blonde hair and with heels was about six foot, one. I had wild, sexy, curly hair and wore the skimpiest dresses. With my larger than life personality, confidence, and no shyness, no one would ever know that I was battling self-esteem issues. If I heard men laughing around me in the clubs, I thought they were laughing at me. The more I would drink, the less I would care and just start to have fun. I was drunk quite a bit. During the days, I worked on my body and made it better and better. This made me feel better about myself. I loved to exercise because it took me out of my head; it made me feel alive and free and empowered. Anytime I felt sad, lonely, angry, frustrated, or stressed, I exercised and felt better.

Throughout college, I read many self-help books and enjoyed studying the mind. I did my very best to love and respect myself and become happier within. I studied psychology, exercise physiology, and anatomy, and I was so intrigued by the human body and mind. I knew that I was getting a great education at top colleges, and I felt like I had a good head on my shoulders. I also knew that I inherited from my dad a gift of being aware of and in tune with your surroundings. I had a gift of being able to accomplish anything that I wanted to do, along with the willingness to put in a lot of effort. It was a gift of never fearing to strive for anything.

My body looked amazing, and my belief in my self-worth was great, but when I looked in the mirror, I still saw the big-eyed, freckle-faced ugly duckling.

I began having a relationship with Jorge at age twenty-four, off and on. Like my dad, he made me feel beautiful and more confident. Unfortunately, we would break up every two to three months and this would tear me apart and make me feel insecure about myself again.

This relationship was very unhealthy and went on for four years. I would not learn until after he passed away that it had more to do with his line of work and less to do with me, but at the time, I blamed myself. This time period was very hard and hurtful, but it also hardened my heart and made me a stronger person. I continued to work on myself by reading, self-talk, and trying to find that inner peace deep in my soul. After Jorge died, I met my husband and had two beautiful children, and this really made me feel beautiful and complete. In my thirties, I began to focus on my family, feel happy, and focus less on myself and my inner feelings.

It wouldn't be until much later that I realized that I was relating happiness to everyone and everything else and not myself. I tried to find happiness with my husband, my kids, and through exercise. It wasn't until I was unable to exercise for eight weeks that I realized I had deeper issues going on internally, issues that I could no longer escape. When my family and friends were not around and I had to sit with myself and my thoughts, there was something very deep going on. I was not letting go of the past, and I was carrying around a ton of baggage and wrongful thinking that was keeping me from moving forward and living the life that I deserved, which was filled with peace and joy and happiness.

Chapter 6

Don't Blame Others for Your Pain

In my late thirties or early forties, I began to feel much more comfortable in my own skin. It was due to a combination of how others made me feel and how I felt about myself. I started to realize that what others felt about me was not all that important to me anymore. What was most important was how I really felt about myself. I had been trying to please and help others for so long that I forgot to please and help myself. I had been working so hard to get the approval of others through my business, my friends, and my family that I lost my sense of self. It started when I was young and wanted to prove myself to my father. This was my fault, not his. I just wanted so badly to be as successful as him, and I was always striving, driving, and pushing myself to prove my self-worth. He was always pushing me to work and be successful, and I felt if I didn't, I would let him down. It was a bit of a double-edged sword because I am so happy he pushed me to drive forward, but I took it to the extreme and was never satisfied with myself because I was not able to be as successful as him. What I was missing was being me. I could not just *be*. I had to keep driving and driving and driving with no end in sight.

When I was a little girl, many of my friends' moms told my mom that their kids could not keep up with me. As an adult, my friends told me to slow down and just relax, and I couldn't do it. I have always been an A type personality, very driven with the go, go, go mentality. I had no problem working fifty hours a week, raising two kids, and working out six days a week. I would keep going until my body would get sick or hurt, and then I would stop temporarily. This went on until I was forty-two years of age.

Even after my heart surgery, I did not slow down one bit. I was always very independent and tried not to ask for help. I could take care of my family, my friends, and myself, and I felt that I needed to do all of this always. Before I had my children, I ran a full marathon and competed in a few fitness competitions. I always pushed my body to the limit, and beyond. After having my kids, I did three more fitness competitions and became very serious with my weight training. I trained five to six times a week with extremely heavy weights, lifting heavier than half of the men in my gym. My OB/GYN told me that due to a tilted uterus and genetics, the heavy lifting had caused my insides to start to collapse. My organs and walls were very weak and

I needed to take it easy and would eventually have to have reconstructive surgery. I said okay and continued to do everything as I always had.

Toward the end of that year, my business partners decided to leave the business in an abrupt manner and we again suffered financially to the point where our landlord owned part of the business. All of this took a toll on me again. My marriage had already gone through three separations, my business took a huge financial loss, and my health was a mess. My doctor told me I must have the surgery within the next couple of months or my organs would fall out of my body. This became very serious.

By mid-December, I had such severe heart palpitations and dizziness that I thought it was my heart issue again. My husband ended up calling 911 at midnight one night to make sure it wasn't my heart. They told me that I was having severe PVCs, which was an irregular heartbeat, but it could just be caused by stress. What they were more concerned with was my blood-sugar level. They tested me and said I might be diabetic, which was extremely unusual! I had just had a slice of pizza, shrimp, and a glass of red wine, so my blood-sugar level should have been normal. They urged me to go straight to my general doctor the next morning because it was extremely low. I drove myself to the doctor the next morning and was feeling horrible. My blood pressure was 137/88, which was extremely unusual for me; I had always had very low blood pressure, averaging 110/65. My doctor was very concerned because of the combination of high blood pressure, low blood-sugar level, and severe heart palpitations, so they sent me next door to the ER. I was in the ER alone for three hours before my husband showed up, and I was very scared. They did all kinds of test and sent me to South Miami to see my heart doctor.

On the car ride there, I was crying to my husband because he chose to sleep in instead of taking me to the doctor in the morning, and this hurt my feelings. As I was in the ER, I was having so many memories of him not being there for my heart surgery and how hurt I was. This only magnified what I was feeling at this moment. He felt that because we were separated at the time of my heart surgery that he did not feel it appropriate to go. I disagreed and still was harboring the hurt, three years later.

It was a very long and stressful day, and I was told that everything was fine. All of my symptoms were caused from stress, and I needed to take some time off and relax. For the first time in my life, I decided to listen to the signs. The universe and God were giving me plenty of warnings, and it was time to listen. I wanted to be healthy and live to see my children grow. I knew that I had a month and a half until my surgery and needed to let my body rest, relax, and get ready for a very serious five-hour surgery. The way I usually prepared for a surgery that would have me out of commission for a while would be very different. I had trained really hard like I was going to compete, so that I could relax and not worry about my body changing after surgery. This time, I finally changed my crazy tactics. I rested and got my body healthy before my surgery. My soul began to talk to me and tell me to listen and be careful of getting hurt.

I had my surgery in February and had to wear a bag to empty my bladder for one week. After a week, I should have been able to empty my bladder on my own, but I could not do it. I was told I could keep the bag for another two weeks or learn how to self-catheterize. If you have ever had to wear a bag, it is not fun because you can't even move around much. I said, "No bag!" I learned how to use the catheters and had to empty my bladder five to six times a day. The first week after my surgery, I was good because I was sleeping all the time and taking pain medication. The second week, I began to read a lot of great self-help books and caught up with friends who came to visit.

By week three, feelings and emotions started to stir up within me about my marriage, my life, my career, my future, everything. I began to realize, at that moment, that in the past when all of these feelings would arise in me, I would go exercise and forget everything. I escaped into a very high-intensity workout and get my endorphins pumping to forget any issues that I was having. I never just sat with my feelings, trying to work through them or listen to my inner voice talk to me. Now, I was not allowed to exercise, so I was forced to sit and think.

I remember my grandmother had a saying that rang true to me. "An idle mind is the Devil's playground." I always believed that, so I always occupied my mind and kept busy. Since I was raised to see the glass half-full, I learned to spin anything negative into a positive. My entire life, I thought that my greatest qualities were my positive and happy nature and that I was a great friend, mother, wife, and helper to everyone. What I never realized was that I did not look within myself to see what I wanted or needed. I was too busy seeing what others needed and wanted. It was time I looked within and found my truth.

Chapter 7

God Will Never
Leave Your Side

My husband spent the night with me at the hospital, the night of my surgery. I was very happy about this due to the past history with him not being there. My mom, who is my best friend, stayed the second night with me. Something very different happened when I came home; my marriage started crumbling once again. I have always been like the caboose on a train in our family, since day one. I was handling the majority of the responsibility in our household, as well as some of the business. Now it was my husband's turn to handle everything the way I had always done. This is where the problem began. He took over the entire business himself. My mom and nanny helped with the kids and I still paid half of all the bills so I thought it would be okay.

I feel that the pressure was not handled well by him, because he was going through his own emotional crisis and did not spend any time with me when I needed him the most. Without time shared and with zero communication, any marriage will fall apart. When I was trying to heal from the surgery, using the catheters and not exercising caused me to be slightly depressed and sad a lot. My friends and parents were a great support— even my children and dog were. The only person who had zero time for me was the one person that I needed the most. I became angry because I felt so neglected and abandoned by the man that I had been with for thirteen years. Since we had separated and reunited three times, I thought that we had overcome most of the obstacles. The ironic thing was that after the surgery, all I wanted and needed was him. In the past, he felt neglected sometimes because I was so strong and independent. Now I was weaker, more vulnerable, and needy, and he didn't know how to handle that side of me.

The fact that those two months had gone by and I still had to use the catheters and could not exercise did not help my emotional state at all. The doctor told me that we would wait one more month and if things did not change, we would do another surgery. I did not want to go back for another surgery, but at least the second one would be much less invasive and only an hour long.

Although I started walking around the neighborhood after week two, it was at a very slow and gentle pace. My body was used to hard-core, high-intensity workouts. By week eight, I was walking ninety minutes a day, but I wasn't getting that endorphin rush that I loved. Exercise had been like a drug to me. My mind continued to be idle, all day long. The universe had literally forced me to face my inner demons and learn how to work through them so that I could finally let them go.

I started to listen to the inner voice that was deep in my soul. I finally realized that a force greater than me had literally kicked my ass to help me up and face the truth. I decided, at this point, to throw my hands up in the air and let go of everything in my life on which I had such a strong grip. I opened my hands, let go, and released everything and anything that wanted to be released. I surrendered to God, the universe, the energy source—each and everything out there that I felt was guiding my spirit to move in a different direction. I believe in God very much, not in a religious sense but in a spiritual one. I was baptized Christian and brought up Jewish and Catholic, but I felt I was just spiritual and would pray at the beach with nature.

During this entire process of letting go, my emotions were like a crazy roller-coaster ride, constantly up and down. For about two to three weeks straight, I felt like I was mildly depressed. I had been sad and low at times in my life, but never continuously and on a daily basis. When Jorge died, and my mom was diagnosed with cancer, I was very sad, but I always had something in my life that made me feel better temporarily. Not this time. I was constantly sad and crying. I felt an enormous lack of control of anything going on in my life. I never felt total despair or severely depressed where I needed medication, but I felt very deep hurt and sorrow, deep in my soul.

My kids were noticing and worried about me. They asked me if I was okay and why I was so sad. I told them it was because of the surgeries and my body being so messed up; they accepted that answer. Although I told them this, I knew that something much greater and deeper was going on internally with my spirit. For the first time in my life, I was facing my truth, my fears, my past, my present, my future, my sorrows, my hopes, and my dreams. Something magically painful was happening, and I had to continue to allow myself to feel all of these emotions. I decided to accept each and every feeling and really feel them in each and every moment. I accepted whatever I was feeling and allowed it to occur without ignoring or dismissing the feelings. In the past, I had always denied them, suppressed them, or exercised them away, and now I sat alone with them and welcomed them. I was not going to put my usual smile on my face and pretend that everything was okay. I was not going to say I was happy when I felt like shit! If certain people in my life didn't like it, tough. I had become selfish and realized that no one else can work through what I am feeling but me.

My husband did not seem to notice the depths of my sorrow because he was living without me. He would say hello and good-bye every day, ask me how I was feeling, and then go about his business. I started back up with the therapist we had seen during our last separation. My husband does not believe in therapy, so we would go for about a month and stop when things got a little better. I started going alone on a weekly basis to try to work through these emotions with a professional. He was such a great therapist, a very New Age-style yoga instructor and family counselor. He was very spiritually minded like me and gave me books to read to help me understand what I was going through. He helped me so much.

I also became friends with a Vedic astrologer from Canada. Pam introduced us, and she was incredible. She would read my chart, but also talk and help guide me to just "Be." Like I said before, I do believe in God. I went to church periodically, but I felt that the rules were too strict for me. I feel that God is in everyone and everything, and he was in me. He was talking, teaching, and guiding me with his Word. I could hear him wherever I was, not just in church. I fully opened myself up to learn and grow. I felt like I was being used like a tool, and every day I had a new lesson, a new sign, and a new path to follow. I listened to the forces surrounding me. I became a full-time student of the universe.

I remember two very impactful moments that occurred and helped me realize that God, the universe, and my spirit were telling me that my destiny was changing toward a new path. After my second surgery to fix my bladder problem, I no longer needed to use the catheters. Two weeks after the surgery, my husband and I got into one of our long and hurtful discussions. He proceeded to tell me that he wasn't going to love me the way I wanted, he wasn't going to go to counseling with me, and he could never make me happy the way

I needed. I was devastated. I was still traumatized from the two surgeries and felt physically and emotionally spent, like there was nothing but sorrow inside of me—and lots and lots of tears. I had been feeling so low and insecure about myself due to using the catheters for three months. I felt so unsexy, like an old woman; this just added to feeling so rejected by him.

I was so distressed that day that I called my therapist to see him for a second time that week. He made me realize that it was a good thing that Matt was telling me what he felt, because in the past, he would just be silent. He also helped me to see that Matt was also going through big emotional issues and I needed to not take it so personally. We both were responsible for our own emotions and actions and needed to continue forward with inner strength.

He convinced me not to cancel my night out to a Bryan Adams concert with my brother and friends. I did not want to go, feeling so down, but I proceeded to put on my sexiest purple dress and go. Would you believe out of 5,000 people at his private acoustic guitar show, he chose me alone to dance while he serenaded me? I was sitting in the row 12 off to the left, and he said, "Girl in the purple dress, stay standing so I can sing to you, and everyone else sit down." Wow, talk about feeling sexy and flattered.

Due to the fact that my brother had bought me two very strong drinks prior to this, I had no problem dancing sexily in front of 5,000 people. After the song, he thanked me and said, "I just have to tell you that you are one beautiful woman!" I knew at that moment that this was not a coincidence; there was a higher power letting me know that I would be okay. I was so excited and happy. I love Bryan Adams, and he really made my night. After the show, I had people taking pictures with me, and they thought that I was part of the show. It was an amazing night and an amazing message.

The second event that occurred was a very rough night at my house. I had gotten so used to being ignored and neglected every night at my house and I would just go in my room and cry. This particular night, I could not stop. I was sobbing hysterically for a long time. I went into my bathroom and knelt down with my hands in prayer position on the closed lid of the toilet and just prayed. I had prayed on my knees a few times in my entire life; this was a tough night that called for it.

I usually said prayers for my family, to keep us together, soften our hearts, make changes, and help things get better. This time, I prayed for myself. I prayed for God and the universe to guide me in the right direction for my destiny. I prayed for peace and joy to enter my heart and soul. I said, "I let go and I will let God guide me, show me, and heal me for what will be best for my future and well-being." Within ten minutes, I felt an overwhelming sense of peace come through me and around me. I felt calmness, stillness, and I started to get chills all up and down my spine. The only time I get these chills in my life is when I know Jorge is around me or I speak or hear the truth deep in my soul. I felt God's presence, and I knew at that moment that I would be okay and continue to move forward. I needed to continue to have faith, hope, and belief.

I knew that my husband was a good man and a good father, but together we're not a good couple. During the times we were separated in the past, we would get along better and be happier within ourselves. I realized that every relationship teaches you something about yourself. They are like reflections in a mirror. I also realized that life is not picture perfect and doesn't always work out exactly the way you thought or hoped it would. We live, we learn, we grow, we experience, we change, and we move on when the time is right. If we continue to change, grow, and move forward, big shifts begin to occur in our lives. Sometimes, these shifts are good, and sometimes, they are bad, but they get us where we need to go. When we have such a strong grip on things that are out of our control, we are not releasing our souls to grow; we are not being guided by our spirit.

When I began to let go of anger and resentment and accept the things I could not change, I started to feel peace. I am thankful to Matt for the good memories we shared, and for giving me two gorgeous and loving children. I wish him nothing but love and happiness, and for him to find the inner peace in his soul as well. Life is a journey of living, loving, and growing, and we must be open to do just that. We must let go and know deep in our souls that a higher power will take us on the right path toward the destination meant for us.

Chapter 8

The Fairy Tale Will Only Confuse You

I was brought up to believe what most little girls do, and that is the fairy tale: be a princess, meet a prince, and live happily ever after. Buy a house with a white picket fence, have kids, and stay married forever, till death do you part. What an absurd fantasy to live by! My parents married young. My mom raised the kids and my dad ran the business, like a typical fairy-tale story. My mom was a wonderful mom dedicated to her family. My dad, also a family man, dedicated his life to providing for the family. My life was like *The Brady Bunch* show on TV. I was very lucky to be raised with so much love, security, and support.

It wasn't until my late teens and early twenties that I started to understand how many issues were going on, which I had been blind too. I began to realize that my parents were not picture perfect and that they were struggling in their marriage. They had both made so many sacrifices to keep our family together. My mom's philosophy was to stay in the marriage for the sake of the children, no matter if she was happy or not. My dad's philosophy was the same, and he thought he was happy also. The truth that I saw was that they both were not happy with each other and were growing apart. My parents did a great job instilling good core values in both my brother and me, but I grew up believing that marriage was for life and you sacrifice your own happiness to keep your family together. I took after both my parents equally. I loved nature and animals and had a loving, feminine side for me and others like my mom. And I was aggressive, driven, and goal orientated like my dad. My dad had a unique belief that I inherited: the good in people always washes away the bad. I was the perfect combination of both parents. Of course, I was not perfect by any means, but I did have some great qualities inherited from each of my parents. They were both great people.

As I was maturing and thinking for myself, I began to realize that life is not a fairy tale. Life is harsh, and it was a continuous struggle toward becoming a better and happier person with all the challenges one must go through. My mom was always a spiritual person who believed in signs from a higher source. My dad was more of a realist; he believed in God but felt that you create and control almost everything in your life. When I got into deep conversations of spirituality, he would call it hocus-pocus, but I couldn't give it up.

When I started studying the human mind and quantum physics, I became intrigued by it all. I believed wholeheartedly in God, the universe, and a source of energy that guided us every step of the way throughout our lives. Through my many experiences—Jorge dying, my friend's coma, my surgeries, my mom's breast cancer, my marriage struggles—I felt as if everything in my life was being played out the way it was meant to be to help me become more of a believer in the higher power. I realized that I needed to completely change my belief system. I tried, but it was a long and endless practice to change the way I had been thinking for all of my life.

When I did marry, I still believed in the white picket fence and the fairy tale, and by no means could any man ever fulfill that fantasy because it was impossible. I had such a strong and unrealistic belief system built up in my head. I do not blame my parents for this belief system. I blame society, the movies, and magazines. Yes, my parents did have a role in my belief system, but they only taught me what they had learned from their parents. It is amazing to me how society distorts reality. We are taught to go to college, get a good job in corporate America, and then work your life away to provide for your family. Yes, we must work hard, and yes, we must provide for our family, but should we sacrifice our lives and our happiness in the interim? So many people are miserable because they are trying to live up to so many expectations of themselves and others. Why are we all so hard on ourselves, and why must we follow this absurd fairy tale that makes us miserable? I did put so many expectations on me and my husband that were unhealthy and unrealistic. It wasn't until I started searching for my truth or my inner voice that things began to change.

I remember back in 2011, when I met my soul sister Pam, I asked her a very important question. "How do you know that your soul is on the right spiritual path?" She always answered with the same response. "You will know, because deep within your core, your truth will tell you." I wanted her to give me the secret, the recipe, a more definite answer with explanations and a road map. Although I respected and loved her, I always doubted her reply. I thought that certain people knew, but I would never be one of them. I was the type of person that thought she heard the truth but would always manipulate the story to get the outcome that she wanted. I never let go of anyone or anything. I held tight to things because of the fear of losing them or letting go of them. For so long, I thought I was listening to my truth or hearing my inner voice, but I was only hearing what I thought I wanted to hear. When I went through all of my health issues and finally decided to surrender and open my hand to let go of anything that was not meant to be with me, my life began to change. It took about two years for me to shift my life and my beliefs and to begin to hear and find my inner truth.

When you start to give up your control and make changes in your life that you are uncertain about, many fears will arise. You will actually start to feel a lot worse before you feel better. I can relate this again to the body. When you get physically hurt, in your back, for example, you rest it, ice it, compress it, massage it, and get therapy, and then it feels worse before it gets better; but the more you do all of these healings and therapies, the better it gets. This is the same with the mind and spirit. The feelings of fear, insecurities, and uncertainties, will all be part of your growing, shifting, and changing toward a more spiritually centered person. Once you silence your mind, listen to your soul, and find your inner truth, the shifts will start to occur and you will begin to find the path to which you were destined.

As I recovered from my two surgeries and started to feel healthier and stronger, I immediately started to make many changes in my life that I felt destined to make. I was able to let go of anger toward my husband for not living out the fairy tale. I began to look at myself very deeply with all of my being. I began to realize that so many of my feelings were of my own doing. I was feeling very insecure, rejected, sad, frustrated, abandoned, and hurt because I myself was going through a difficult period in my life.

I took charge of myself and decided to really be open to each and every feeling that I felt. I was much easier on me and far less judgmental than I had ever been. I knew that only I could make me feel all of those feelings. Another person cannot make us feel a certain way; we do that to ourselves. There was something deep in my soul that I still needed to work through to find my truth. All of these feelings were dwelling deep inside me from my childhood and my beliefs of myself. I needed to work through each feeling, one-by-one, and understand why I felt them. Once I figured out why they were there, I could release them and move on. This is not at all an easy task, but it is something that must be done in order to find the truth of your spirit.

I am not blaming myself for my marriage failing; of course, it takes two people. I was just taking charge of my life and myself in order to heal. Once I reached a point of zero hope and zero expectations from anyone but myself, I was able to grow and take full responsibility for my own feelings. My husband and I were brought together for a reason to learn and grow together. We did learn a lot from each other, and we grew apart. In some relationships, you learn and continue to grow together in a healthy, positive way, and in others, when your growth stops, your relationship ends. When I understood this, I was able to let go and finally move forward without guilt or regret. At that point, I went from the belief system of keeping the family together for the sake of my kids, to ending the relationship for the sake of my kids. Children thrive from two happy parents that give love and security, not from an unhappy household filled with tension and stress. It took four separations, loads of therapy, self-therapy, and reading to reach this point of letting go of my marriage. Once I decided to give myself love, respect, and worth on a much higher level, I was able to walk away and know that I could not fix something that had been broken for so long.

Once you let go of the false belief systems—release everything and truly surrender to the universe—the universe will not fail you. I can share now with all you self-doubters and naysayers who don't believe you will find your true spiritual path that *you will*. You will find your path, but it will take a lot of hard work, discipline, time, and practice to be able to learn, grow, and hear your truth. Pam was right: you will know, and it will not be easy. No one can give you the magic recipe; you must find it for yourself by letting go of the fairy tale and having faith.

Chapter 9

The Right People Will Be Brought into Your Life, When Needed

Amazing occurrences began to happen in my life when I finally moved out of my house, sold my business, and left my husband. I began to have many dreams and would actually hear God speak to me. The entire universe opened up for me and guided me every step of the way. I was being led on a new path. This path had so many signs, encouraging words, and people to help me along the way.

Although I was scared and uncertain about all aspects of my future, I felt this calm, inner peace that I had never felt before. I remember waking up one morning in my new house and hearing a song in my head. It was so clear and vivid, and I knew the song, but I had really never listened to the words on the radio before this. The song said, "Don't you worry, child. Heaven's got a plan for you." Amazing. The most amazing thing was that I woke up three days in a row hearing the same verse to the same song. I always believed in things happening in threes, and this surely made me feel so assured that I was doing the right thing. I woke up each day filled with such peace and hope that everything was going to be okay.

Upon my new spiritual development, I met so many great teachers. I met people who were going through, or who had been through, similar situations, and they shared their experiences with me. I felt that once I stopped trying to please others and get acceptance from them, many of those individuals disappeared and new ones appeared. I feel that our souls are connected to other people depending on the energy we are exuding and the paths we are on in our lives. It doesn't matter in what part of the world these souls are; if we are meant to meet them, we will.

Throughout my transitional period of resettling in my new life, I met just such a significant person that made a huge impact on my life. Since I am a fitness professional, I connect with thousands of fitness professional on my Facebook page because we network and share tips with one another. I had been on Facebook for six months but never really reached out to any of them, just read and learned from some of the best in our industry. One day I happened to stumble upon a picture of a very successful fitness professional that lived completely across the map from me, in another country. I admired his picture because of his cool hockey jacket and his cute daughters. I started reading his posts about his success in fitness and his passion, drive, goals, and ambitions. He was very motivational and inspiring, to the point where I felt that his posts on Facebook were feeding my soul with exactly what I needed to get through this rough period of my life. I never once thought of him as a man to date, although he was very good-looking. I looked at him as a mentor or a guide that was put into my life for a higher purpose. I felt that my soul knew his in a way that was so familiar to me. His posts would awaken the higher part of me that was filled with strength and passion for life. I admired his strength, his words, his family values, his accomplishments, and his zest for life. I just loved his pictures with his gorgeous and happy daughters; the three of them were so close. On some of my hardest days, I found strength and encouragements in the words he shared on his Facebook page. On days of sadness or sorrow, he would post happy, uplifting posts.

One particular night, I went to bed with a very sad and heavy heart about my kids missing their dad. I felt guilty that I was depriving them of the family life. In the morning, when I turned on my computer, before opening my Facebook page, I prayed for God to give me strength to get through the day and help me know that I was doing the right thing. This man's post was the first to appear on my screen. It was such a gorgeous picture of him on the water with his daughters. He was sharing how he wanted to thank the mother of his daughters for helping him to raise two loving and wonderful girls. He shared how even though they raised them separately, with love and security they had come out so well adjusted. A woman wrote a post thanking him and shared how she was going through a divorce and scared for her kids. He reassured her and told her that as long as both parents remained friends and gave the kids love and support, they would be fine. I felt at that moment that God and the universe had placed this person in my life to help guide me and show me the way.

I decided to send him a private message thanking him for his posts of encouragement, motivation, and inspiration. I told him briefly about my love for fitness and helping others, my work with Pam and genetics, and my dream to write a book. He shared with me how he felt he had a calling from God at age eight to do something of great importance to help heal the world. Funny, because I felt the same and had a calling from God at age five. Women mature faster than men, so my calling was at a younger age, I told him with a chuckle. We became friends and continued to stay in touch.

It wasn't until a month later that I saw an article that his friend had written about him and his battle with cancer. I was shocked.

While reading the story, tears filled my eyes because it was such an inspiring story. He had been asymptomatic and pushed the doctors to test him for months. They found a baseball-sized tumor that was a stage 4 cancer. It was behind his nose and throat, close to his brain. Instead of giving up, he fought long and hard through chemo and radiation and beat the cancer. Two years later, he is living life to the fullest. I found this story so compelling because he shared that with a positive mind-set and a healthy lifestyle, one can overcome anything. I truly believe this with all of my heart and soul.

My friend now teaches people how to eat whole, organic foods and drink lots of organic juices. He speaks all over the world about his trials and tribulations and how to live life to the fullest through mind-set, nutrition, and exercise. This man is an amazing individual who continues to inspire and motivate others. He is living out his calling from God and it is beautiful.

I had the honor to meet him and his daughters, and I thoroughly enjoyed being in their presence. People like this are so enjoyable to be around because they bring love and light to the world. He helped me a great deal in my life and did not even know it. He inspired and motivated me to keep moving forward on my path. "Do not stay stuck" and "Do not doubt" were the messages I learned from him. I find it truly amazing how the universe puts people in your life and on your path at the exact moment that you need them the most. All of our souls our connected in one way or the other, and if you let go of controlling your destiny, the right souls will find you. Thank you, Peter, for your guidance, inspiration, mentorship, and friendship.

I also reconnected with a very spiritual individual that had been important in my life back when I was dating Jorge, fourteen years prior. The CD that I found at that time, the one that helped me come up with the name of the gym, was created by a man named John Traficante. This was the CD that helped me heal through losing Jorge and the one that appeared while I was writing this book ten years later. I reached out to John on Facebook and shared the spiritual connections that I had with him and the CD. We spoke for hours and decided that we would collaborate in the future with healing and teaching seminars. We both agreed that we were brought back into each other's lives for a higher purpose and we needed to acknowledge that our reconnection was meant to happen. He sent me his latest book, *Total Reboot of Your Soul.* I read the entire book in a couple of days, and—wow—it helped me a great deal to put everything into perspective regarding what was happening to me on this spiritual journey. We both feel so strongly that our voices are meant to be heard and that we need to share our stories with the world.

Everyone has a voice, and everyone can help heal others with their own experiences in life. There are so many people in pain who don't know how to deal with it. So many turn to alcohol, illegal drugs, and prescription pills as an escape. When I mention to people that I am writing a book, many ask, "What will make your book successful?" It is not about making my book successful. It is about helping others to heal. Everyone could write a book about their experiences in life. Everyone has a voice that needs to be heard. It is about sharing your experiences, your ups and downs, joys and sorrows, your pains, challenges, goals, and accomplishments. You can share how you overcame pain, your coping methods, and your stories of love and loss. Everyone has a story that can shed light to others.

Life is all about choices. Many people will make bad choices because they are not educated and do not know how to deal with certain situations. I am hoping to help people by sharing my experiences. I want to show how to help others make better choices, to choose love over fear, health over drugs, and happiness over pain. This is what I hope to help people begin to understand: we have choices. Choose to be happy and healthy. Feed your mind with positive affirmations. Feed your body with good, nutritious food, and surround yourself with like-minded people. One of my favorite quotes was from Tosca Reno, the founder of *Oxygen* magazine. "With a positive mind-set, your body will react accordingly." I loved this because, no matter how much you work out and eat healthily, if your mind is in an unhealthy state, your body will fail. You must nurture your mind, body, and spirit to be at your best.

You can manifest anything into your life by just believing and living out those thoughts. I knew as a little girl that I wanted to own a business by age thirty. I also wanted to get married and have a family around the same age. I wanted two kids: a girl and a boy. I manifested all of this into being. Anything I have ever wanted within my own life, I have imagined, believed, and manifested.

My challenge was letting go of constant control of getting what I want in the timing that I wanted, not what God wanted for me. I had very little patience. I needed to learn to let go and stop holding on with such tight reigns. Even if I had always believed and had faith that what is meant to be would be, I needed to learn to be patient and know that what I needed would come.

When I started working out at age seventeen, it was always high-intensity workouts: spinning, step, running, weight training, intervals, skiing, and biking. I could never sit still long enough for yoga, Pilates, or meditation; they were too slow and boring for me. On the cruise that I took my mom in 2011, I met a unique woman who shared her story with me and how yoga saved her life. She had endured much violence, abduction, and drugs throughout her life, and after rehab, yoga helped her heal inside herself. I went riding with her on one of the islands. We had hours to talk on our trail ride, and within those hours, it was so peaceful and relaxing; we really bonded.

I made a promise to her that I would give yoga a try when I returned to Florida. It would not be hard for me to find yoga classes because my gym offered at least ten classes a week; there was no excuse. The class I chose was a seniors-level gentle yoga. I figured that I had enough intense exercise, so I would take a relaxing, gentle-stretching and meditation yoga. I fell in love with the class! I enjoyed and needed so desperately the stretching and the meditation at the end put me into a state of total relaxation.

I continued to take the class two times a week for months, and this class opened up a new door in my

Lisa Dwoskin

knowledge of mind-body connection. I began to explore all the different meditation teachers. I found that many of my favorite authors also had CDs for meditation. One of my favorites was Brian Weiss's *Eliminate the Stress Meditation*. This CD took me into a different world; I completely fell into a deep state of relaxation and started to love to meditate. It was definitely a process of practice, discipline, and consistency to reach the deep relaxation, but it was so worth it. I started out with ten to twenty minutes a day because my mind would wander and it would be hard to just relax, but after a while, I wanted and needed it more and more. Sometimes, I just fell asleep because I was so relaxed. It was incredible. I read that some experts thought it was not good to fall asleep, but I felt that if I was so relaxed that I fell asleep, it was a good thing. At times, I would just be in a sleep-like state where my mind was at rest but I was semi-awake; this was a deep relaxation. At the time I was learning to meditate, I rescued a six-month-old black Labrador, and she meditated with me. It was so funny. Five minutes into the CD, she would start snoring, so I guess it works for animals as well.

I honestly never thought I would be one of those people that could sit still long enough to learn how to meditate. I certainly never thought I would be able to silence my mind long enough to fall into a deep relaxation, but I did. Meditation became a huge part of my life and helped me on my path toward spiritual enlightenment. Many things are seen and heard while you are in a state of deep relaxation. When you are able to quiet your mind, you are able to hear God speak to you. Some feel that it is their spirit guides, angels, or the universe, and I feel I can hear God in a way that I could not hear in my everyday busy life. It is not like a conversation with a friend but more like an internal voice that helped guide me in the right direction. The more I meditated, the more I had dreams at night when I slept. It was as if I had opened a new door into the higher powers of the universe. I began to listen to other CDs on guided imagery and self-visualization, which are other ways to meditate. It is an ongoing process of knowledge and practice, and I loved every moment of it all.

Many people began to appear in my life who had not been there before, almost like guides for me. People who had been in my life had begun to disappear, people who were on different paths from me. Every day, I became more peaceful and felt lighter with more joy and happiness. I had discovered a way to help me feel better by looking within instead of externally; this was a big transition for me. I feel that we are all souls roaming around and trying to search for the light, the peace, joy, and happiness.

What we need to realize is that all of this is within us and around us, and we need to be still to comprehend this. We allow society, rules, regulations, false beliefs and realities, fantasies, and other people to guide us and create us throughout our lives. We try to control all aspects of our lives, please others, and live by others' opinions of us, and none of this helps us. It only hurts us. I lived half of my life asking everyone their opinion before I would make my own decision about parts of my life. If I did not like their opinion, I would manipulate the story to get the opinion I was looking for.

At forty-two years of age, I finally stopped listening or caring about what others thought or said about me. Once I began to let go of all my false beliefs and let go of hope or expectations or outcomes, I was free. I was free to just be me. Every day, I had a sign or was reassured by my higher powers that I was on the right path. My soul felt like it had been released after being tied down and suppressed for so long. This is when my true journey began.

Chapter 10

Spiritual Workouts

There are always stumbling blocks along your journey to get to wherever you are going. With me, my path was toward a higher level of spiritual enlightenment. Remember anything worth achieving takes hard work and dedication to get there. Nothing comes easily; it takes a lot of effort to achieve your goals.

The simplest way for me to describe my spiritual workouts is to compare them to my physical workouts. When I was seventeen years old, I became a workout fanatic, and I have never stopped. I exercise every day of my life and love every minute of it. It takes dedication to get your butt moving every day, even when you don't feel like it. I have such a strong passion for exercise—both doing and teaching it. I tell people that exercise to me is like brushing my teeth; it is something I do every day without thinking about it. Working out makes me feels so good externally and internally, and I look forward to doing it as often as possible.

I love to feel good and healthy psychologically as well, and I get this temporarily from the high of exercise. In order to have the mental peace long-term, this also takes work. Why do so many people exercise their bodies but not their minds as well? Along my journey of transforming my mind and soul, I have run into many challenges. It has not been easy by any means.

My mind likes to be in opposition to my soul. Throughout my life thus far, my mind has always overpowered my soul. It is not easy to transition your being to living a spirit-centered life, compared with an ego-centered one. The ego, which is our mind, tries to run our lives with constant control and manipulative thoughts. The ego causes you to have thoughts of anger, sadness, depression, negativity, competition, criticism, guilt, pride, and self-sabotage. The spirit teaches you to let go and just be in the moment, feel peace, love, joy, and happiness. The spirit does not want you to judge or criticize yourself, just to love and accept yourself. Why is it so hard for people to live from the spirit and not from the ego?

Years and years of conditioning have taught us to live such mediocre lives instead of lives filled with abundance of all areas of life. No one is a perfect human being. We all need to learn, grow, and overcome many obstacles in life. It is how we choose to do this that matters. We need to accept the hardships that come our way and understand that these obstacles are here to teach us to grow, change, and make our futures brighter. Once we let go of our fear and embrace change, we grow and become better individuals. Change is scary, but change is necessary.

When you have faith and believe in a higher power, you will let your fears go and accept the changes that are occurring around you. In a matter of one month, I sold my business, filed for divorce, moved to a new house, and changed my children's school. I was filled with fear, but I did not let it hold me back. Instead, I embraced it and kept moving forward. It took time to let go of what was so familiar to me for the past thirteen years, and it was scary. I had allowed myself for so long to hang on tightly to whatever I had in my life because of fearing the unknown. After so many signs and occurrences from the universe, I decided to let go and take the leap of faith into the unknown. I decided to take my life one day at a time, moment-by-moment and step-by-step. I had been such an organized woman my entire life. I used to preplan every event in my life, often years prior to them happening. The good news was that I was able to manifest almost anything I wanted, but the bad news was I never let go and allowed life to just happen without a plan.

The hardest part of my journey was accepting the instability, uncertainty, and lack of structure that had become my new life. I had no idea what the outcome would be, and I felt lost at times. This is when I would see my therapist. He reflected back how I felt so vividly. He told me that it was as if I were treading water in the middle of the ocean, never knowing what would happen next and just trying to stay afloat. Do you give up and drown, or do you keep going and have faith that the outcome will be good?

I had conditioned myself for so many years to be a creature of habit. My work, kids, and husband had become my identity, and I just kept going day to day, whether happy or not, because I thought this was what my life was meant to be. All of a sudden, I was no longer a businesswoman or a wife, and it was strange to accept. I was still a mother, but when the kids were in school, I would allow my mind to race with the unanswered questions. What will I do with myself? What will my next career move be? Will I love and be passionate about what I do? Will I date? Will I fall in love again? Will the man that I meet like my kids? Will I be happy with a man that is not my children's father? Will I make enough money to survive? Will my kids be happy? On and on, my mind would race and analyze, driving me crazy. I knew that I needed to channel my energy and bring peace to my mind and spirit if I wanted to grow, and this is when I decided to commit to my spiritual practice the way I did to my physical exercise.

I started every morning with my physical workout, either a long walk or jog on the beach or an intense gym workout with weights. I loved the walks on the beach because I really could connect with nature; the birds, trees, sky, and ocean truly soothed my soul. After training or teaching for a few hours, I went home to meditate. Depending on my time availability, I meditated fifteen to sixty minutes at a time. I always put on music, either just nature music or a guided meditation, to help my mind shut off and not get cluttered with chatter. I would wake up to feeding my mind with positive affirmations and continue to read short, positive quotes at least three to five times a day. I also was always reading a book on spiritual enlightenment, at least one chapter or more a day.

At this time, I chose to do one or more acts of kindness on a daily basis, with or without my kids. We would buy food or water for homeless people, take kids without parents for a few hours, or volunteer in any way we could. All of these daily practices filled my mind and spirit in such a positive way. When you are feeding yourself with these things on a daily basis, it is almost impossible not to move forward and feel better. There was no time to dwell and have negative thoughts, and when few thoughts would try to creep in, I would redirect them immediately. This is when your life begins to change.

There were still definitely hard days when my old patterns would come back to haunt me and I allowed them to do so. I allowed myself to feel the hurt, pain, sadness, and loss because I knew that I could not deny myself a grieving period. I had been married to my business and husband for thirteen years and you don't just get over that so easily. My husband and I shared many beautiful memories that were not easy to let go of, and he was a large part of my life. It is good to feel your pain, work through it, and then let it go. It is not good to hold onto things and forever be the victim of your pain. It was a long and slow process, but day-by-day, it got easier to let go and move forward.

In order to grow spiritually, you must continue to feed your mind and spirit in a positive way and let your ego go. A person does not lose fifty pounds overnight, and you cannot change your mind that quickly either. It takes months to lose weight and become fitter and healthier, and it takes longer to reprogram your mind. Both mind and body take time to get fitter and healthier. Once you do lose the weight, and do change your thoughts, it is something you must continue on a regular basis. It is not something that just happens and then you give up and expect to stay the same. My body is in great shape because I have been eating healthy and exercising for most of my life. Now, my mind and spirit have grown and become much healthier and happier. I need to continue my practice and exercises for my whole life.

Along your journey, what you find will be not at all what you expected. You will find that the things you thought made you happy really do not. Once you let go of control and let your spirit guide you, you will discover things about yourself that you never knew existed. When you expand your wings and begin to fly, your path will lead you in directions you would have never gone down. When our spirits show us the path along the way, you must free your mind and continue moving forward in that direction that you are meant to be traveling. You will not regret surrendering and letting God guide the way.

Chapter 11

Cleansing Your Mind, Body, and Spirit with Juicing

As a former fitness competitor, I consumed large amounts of meat and protein on a daily basis. I ate a lot of chicken breasts, lean, ground turkey, and regular meat, fish, sweet potatoes, and brown rice, and I drank many protein shakes. This book is not a book on diet and nutrition, but I must slightly touch on food consumption. What we put in our bodies affects our minds, bodies, and spirits so much. If you are going to embark on this spiritual journey with me, you must take a serious look at your menu and diet. When I say the word *diet*, I am not referring to a cutback; I am referring to a way of life in the way you eat. A very dear friend of mine, who is also a personal trainer, referred to a diet as a menu plan. What does your menu plan look like?

If you are feeding your body with junk, you are filling your mind and spirit with junk as well. Have you ever noticed that when you feed your body good, clean, nutritious food, your spirit comes alive and you think so much more clearly? I remember so many of the competitions I trained for. Back then, when I had to lower my carbs to nearly nothing, I could barely concentrate. Our bodies need to be fed properly in order to function properly. When I became more interested in all aspects of spiritual growth, I was noticing so much more information on plant-based diets and what they are doing to our foods with pesticides and hormonal abuse. At one of my Hay House events, I had the pleasure of listening to Kris Carr. Wow! She was amazing and so knowledgeable about juicing and eating for cell regeneration and longevity of life. I bought her book *Crazy Sexy Diet* and really learned the proper ways to prepare fruits and vegetables that are healthy for the body.

My Facebook friends were also sharing loads of information on eating meat and animal abuse and how unhealthy it all has become. When you start changing your life, information is brought to you when you are ready and open to hear it. My father's girlfriend, who is my close friend, has been trying to educate me on these topics for years, but I was not ready to make the change in my life. As my spiritual growth took over my life, these aspects became so much more important to me. Not only did I start to change the way that I ate, I also changed my workouts. I slowly transitioned to safer and gentler exercises and not such hard-core, heavy lifting. Meditation, yoga, Pilates, walking, and eating better all go hand-in-hand.

I decided with the help of Kris Carr's book to try a juice cleanse for three to seven days, depending on how I felt. I recommend you do a one-day cleanse, but for me, I wanted more. I love challenges, and I am a much disciplined individual. I do everything more extremely than the average person. I also know my body very well, and I am very educated in being careful with electrolytes, calories, fat, protein, and carbs. I was going to take a week off from exercise to let my body have a rest and start juicing. I was hoping to get a spiritual, euphoric feeling as well. I had been through so many changes recently so I thought this would really bring me to a higher level.

I used the recipes out of the book that were so delicious: a green juice and a green smoothie. I started day one with just juicing, but I added a vegan protein powder in each juice. I was a little concerned that I didn't want to drop my protein so low because my body was used to large amounts of protein to maintain my muscle mass. Day 2 was the same, but at night, I added a smoothie, which was yummy. It had avocado and a banana and it felt so much thicker and fuller. Days 1 and 2, I felt good. By day 3, I dropped the protein powder and started really detoxing. I was in the bathroom half of the day, but I felt good. Day 4, I was lethargic but waiting for the euphoric feeling. I was told by day 5, I would feel so great. I was feeling many highs and lows with being tired and foggy in the brain. Day 5 was not good for me; I had nausea and headaches and was very tired. It probably didn't help that I was menstruating, had a very stressful day, and had not slept the night before because of a sick kid. I decided day 6 to add some hummus and almond butter to my fruit and veggies. I knew that I had to ease back into eating again, so I decided to stay on a plant-based menu for a couple of more weeks.

I am very happy that I tried juicing because it opened my eyes to how important organic fruits and vegetables are as the staple of our menu plan. I found great recipes from the book on how to cook for my family and eat nutritiously for my brain and soul. I will continue to juice once a day as part of my menu because it is so good for you and tastes delicious—at least I think so. If I do decide to eat meat again, which I am sure I will, I will definitely be more conscious of my choices and buy organic meats. I never reached that euphoric state, but I did feel good on all but that one day. My kids said that I was extremely moody, which I do not deny. I am used to exercising every day and feeling energized from that. My body needs more food, not just juice.

What I did learn during the process is very similar to what my entire spiritual journey has taught me. It is not about finding that euphoric state; it is about being in the moment. I have learned to just be—not high high and not low low. What is fascinating is that I felt good throughout, the same way my life has been playing out. I felt peaceful and relaxed most of the time, and that is wonderful. I truly believe that we have so much power over our lives simply with our minds. My mind told me to keep going, and I did. The best part of the juicing process for me was meditating every day for one hour and reaching a deeper spiritual level; this did happen. I was more relaxed and really could silence my mind and connect with my God source. So in this respect I found my euphoric state.

Chapter 12

Manifesting Your Dreams

It is so true that our minds can control our entire lives by manifesting anything that we desire, if it is in our best interest and takes us to our highest state of existence. Ever since I was a little girl, I have manifested anything that I have ever desired and more, and in the exact order that I had intended. As I got older, I found it so fascinating how a thought in your mind became a feeling in your body, and when the words were spoken, the action would occur.

There are many great books that helped guide my belief and direction in manifesting abundance into my life. Two great books I read were *The Power of Intention* by Wayne Dyer and *The Secret* by Rhonda Byrde. Throughout the thirteen years that I owned my business, whenever I needed something or someone, I would just think it, feel it, say it, and it would come to pass. When I had my heart issue, I did the same exact thing. I never once believed anything but the fact that my heart would be fixed and I would be healthy. I thought it, believed it, felt it, and said it every day until I was perfectly healthy. Of course, there were days of self-doubt and hardships and days where my thoughts were not properly aligned, and I knew they weren't because those were the harder and more trying days for me.

Like I said before, spiritual enlightenment is an ongoing process. Negative thoughts will try to creep into everyone's mind once in a while. It is how we learn to deal with these thoughts more effectively that matters. The longer you practice positivity and living a spirit-centered life, the quicker the negative thoughts will disappear. In order to manifest abundance into your life, your thoughts have to be aligned with your feelings. The universe knows when you are speaking the positive thoughts but not feeling or living in them. Many people get so frustrated when they cannot manifest good things into their lives. These people talk the talk but do not walk the walk. This means that they are preaching and saying the words, but their thoughts and feelings are saying something different. We can all talk a great game. The question is this: can you truly live the same way?

I love the scenario of the people who go to church or temple for a couple hours a week, but when they leave, they commit every sin and harm and hurt others on a daily basis. In order to manifest abundance of all good things in your life, you must be living a life filled with abundance. You must give love to others without expecting anything in return, whether you have money or not. The people that give kindness to others, only to receive something in return, will never get it.

I think the problem with many people is that they do not love themselves enough to be capable of loving others. Louise Hay has the best approach to learning to love yourself. Start your day with looking at yourself in the mirror and simply saying, "I love you." Self-love is the most sacred love of all, because without it, you can never be happy with yourself or others. A very strong emotion that we all have is guilt that stops us from truly loving ourselves. Guilt for everything in life: actions we did, regrets we cannot let go of, mistakes in childhood or adulthood, etc. Guilt stops us from accepting ourselves as we are. We need to forgive ourselves, be kind to ourselves, and love ourselves in order to grow.

I went to dinner with a friend one night. As we were watching the sunset, enjoying some wine, we covered some very heavy topics about life. She was expressing to me the tough times she was going through in her marriage, job, and self and about her childhood struggles. Her biggest challenge was growing up with lack of love and support and feeling guilty about everything that occurred to her throughout her life. She continuously blamed herself for everything and anything bad that happened to her. She has never played the victim card and has grown into a very successful businesswoman that makes a very high income for her family, but she is not happy. She became so accustomed to doing for everyone but herself that she has very little self-love and self-worth. Instead of loving herself and being kind to herself, she kept blaming herself for everything and became overcome with guilt that she wanted more. She has moved cities and jobs several times, and none of these changes made her happier, because she needs to dig deep internally and begin to love herself more.

We talked for three hours about self-love and self-acceptance, and we both agreed that it is so hard for women to let go of trying to make everyone happy and focus on their own self-worth. My friend is a brilliant, highly educated woman that just needed someone else to point out to her what she was not seeing for herself. It was interesting because we had been childhood friends who had gotten so caught up with life that we hadn't spent much quality time together for a while. We were both similar women who went through most of our lives helping and healing others. When it came down to ourselves, we were quick to judge when others tried to tell us what we needed to improve on. Through a lot of maturing and growing, we were able to have an open and honest conversation about life and spiritual enlightenment. I was very grateful that night to share with her my journey and how much I have learned about becoming more in touch with my inner spirit. She was very inspired by my growth and how I shared it with her, and she was very proud of how far I had come.

This particular night reassured me that the universe had a much bigger plan for me. I was not only placed on this path for my own spiritual growth, I was put here to help guide others in a similar direction. Since that night, I have come across so many women who are struggling with so many issues in their lives and do not know where to turn. I do not have all the answers, but I can share with these women my journey, what I have been through, and what has helped me.

Before starting my journey and transformation, I was just as lost and confused as so many others. I knew about spirituality and self-help books. I had read and educated myself enough to know how to try to be positive over negative. What I didn't know was how to truly live a spirit-centered life on a day-to-day basis and how much dedication, discipline, and effort it would take to get there. I also did not realize that once you think you are there, you truly are not; you are probably only halfway there. The real work starts once you have arrived, it is a never-ending process of learning, educating, and growing. The good news is it is a wonderful and beautiful process of growth, which changes you.

Spiritually enlightened people are wonderful, loving, giving, caring, and compassionate. These are the people who can move mountains and change lives. Once the door is opened for you, there is no turning back because you have found the secret. The secret to life, to living, to peace, and to happiness is to give, to love, to be kind, and to help educate others to learn and do the same. This is also for men; it is just usually the women who express their needs and wants more, but men can surely benefit as well.

Chapter 13

Gratitude

When you wake up in the morning, you must be grateful and thankful for everything in your life, whether big or small or good or bad. Feed your mind with positive thoughts from the moment you open your eyes. After I say my morning prayers and give thanks to God, I turn on my computer and start to read my news feed on Facebook. I have many health and wellness people on my page, and they post such beautiful and spiritual messages that are very uplifting to start my day. Some posts are about exercise, some are about God, and some are just positive affirmations, but none are negative. They are all meant to bring motivation to start your day off great.

As I was taking my long walk on the beach this morning, I felt nothing but gratitude. It was raining lightly and there was not one person out on the beach; I felt like I was on a deserted island. It was so peaceful and quiet. After listening to the ocean and birds for a while, I decided to listen to my iPod music with my headphones. A song I love, Lynyrd Skynyrd's "Freebird," was playing, so I started smiling and singing loudly, enjoying every minute of it. As I walk, I usually look straight ahead or out at the ocean. I don't usually look down; however, something drew my eyes down, and I saw an amazing message in the sand. It was a big giant heart with the infinity symbol drawn inside of the heart; it was beautiful. The tractor had already been flattening the sand and the tide was very high, so I guess the universe wanted me to see this before it got washed away. I stopped and took a picture of it because it moved me in a way of great significance. I interpreted this as infinite love, which is what we are all about.

Giving and receiving love is what makes this universe a better place. As I continued my walk, I was filled with peace, love, and hope for a wonderful life and future. Being grateful for every moment we are alive is a must if you want to live a happy and fulfilled life. We are all so blessed to be able to wake up every morning and *live*.

Each and every one of us has hardships in our lives. We have negative feelings and thoughts, and this is normal. What we need to do is fill our days with more good than bad. In order to have more joyous days, we need to be grateful for just being. As I continue to grow along my spiritual path, I do have bumps in the road, and that is okay. I accept myself fully—good and bad, happy and sad. When I think of memories of my husband, my family together, Jorge being alive, and many more, I feel them and let them go. I no longer dwell on them and reminisce on them for too long, or wish that I had them again. Now, I accept that it was my past and I look forward to what my future holds.

I used to fear my future and want to go back to my past, because it was certain. The uncertainty of the future scared me so much that I would hold on to the past. Now, I understand that with love and faith, there is no need to fear the future or let go of the past; it is a process called life. Every memory was meant to be a part of my journey that has led me to where I am now. Every person, place, and thing was meant to be in my life, and who is meant to stay, stays. Those who are meant to leave, leave. It is destiny. I will continue to make the twist and turns that life is showing me and I will follow the direction. I just take a few deep breaths and let go. I have faith that the universe knows what it is doing, and so does God. I continue moving forward every day, and I continue to strengthen the spiritual path that is guiding me.

Breathing is so important for so many reasons. Deep breathing can bring you from a high anxiety state to a very calm and soothing one. Many people take drugs for anxiety, when all they really need is to breathe slowly, lower their heart rate, and center their minds, bodies, and spirits. When I do my deep breathing, I close my eyes and imagine breathing in all the white, pure energy around me. Then as I exhale, I release all the bad and negative energy that could be around me. Other times, I will take a long, deep breath, hold it for four to five seconds, and then slowly exhale to calm myself down. All you need is three or four rounds of this breathing technique to calm your nervous system down and relax your mind. It truly works.

My children also use these breathing exercises when they get upset and need to calm down. My son is seven years old and the breathing is the only thing that relaxes him when he gets angry or has a temper tantrum. Sometimes, they get so mad at me and say, "No, I will not do your stupid deep breaths," but then they do, and it always works. It is so important for us to teach our children alternative methods than the usual yelling, spanking, or punishing to get them to listen. My kids have been taught to love nature and be grateful for everything that life has to offer. They come with me to do volunteer work and help the homeless, and they love it. My kids are seven and eight years old, and they love to help people and spread the love. My son loves to talk to me about God, the sun, the sky, and the moon. I have taught him about the full moon and new moon, and we even do rituals with the intentions and the candles that each new moon brings.

Both kids love to think positive thoughts. They teach their friends that you could turn your day around by just speaking or feeling better. My daughter is such an artistic free spirit. She loves nature, animals, and helping kids with special needs. She fights with other kids and tells them not to make fun of people or bully kids. When my kids come home from school, the first thing we do is sit and I listen about their day. They tell me the good and bad and everything in-between. I make sure I listen with undivided attention and give them eye contact so they know I truly want to hear what they have to say. When they talk about mean kids, I try to make them see that maybe those kids are going through rough times in their homes or are taught bad values.

I also teach my kids about ego versus spirit. They might not grasp the concept, but they listen and try to understand. I explain to them that they need to send love and light even to the mean kids because they might need it. They need to learn to not take things so personally and understand that it is not about them; it is about whatever is happening in the child's life at the time. When I talk about ego, I place my hand on their heads, and when I talk about spirit, I place my hand on their hearts. The connection to head and heart helps them. I don't expect my kids to be perfect, but I do want them to learn about spiritual enlightenment, and I try to lead by example.

My son had a great learning experience a couple of weeks ago while waiting for me at a local studio where I was teaching a spinning class. It was my first time at this high-end yoga, Pilates, and spinning studio. I was subbing for another instructor. The instructor was a very good-looking man, and he was the owner of the studio, so the clients loved him. The class was full and no one knew that he was not coming. The clients pay per class and it is not cheap, so they want a great workout. I have been teaching for twenty years and am very good at what I do, but you will not know this until you experience my class. Unfortunately, some people do not even want to give anyone else a chance. After many people asked me where the instructor was and if I was teaching, I stood in front of the class and told them that I was teaching and I was great at what I did. I said, "Take the class, and you will love it!"

Three minutes into the class, just as I started to tell everyone what to do, one lady stormed out visibly upset and unhappy. I ignored her and continued to start the class and make everyone happy.

Five minutes later, the lady came back in with the owner and they both got on bikes and took the class. The owner stayed about twenty minutes and told me he loved the class, and the angry lady ended up staying for the entire class, as did everyone else. They were so pleased that many asked the owner to give me a permanent class. I was not surprised, because I know I am a great instructor and I love what I do, so it shows.

My son had been playing on his iPad at the juice bar the entire time I was teaching my class. As we got in the car and left the gym, my son was so eager to tell me about the angry woman. He told me that she was yelling at the owner and telling him that she refused to take anyone else's class and that she wanted to quit the gym and get her money back. My son was so worried that I was upset or that my feelings were hurt from this woman. He asked me how come I was not mad. I explained to him that not everyone will always like you, and that is okay. I told him that the lady did not even want to open her heart or mind to try my class from the start, and even if she took the class and hated it, that would be okay too. I explained to him further how people prejudge you before they even know you. This is the case for homeless people, special-needs people, and many others who have issues we don't even know about. Then I brought up the lesson about other kids who act this way and how he cannot let it get him upset. I told him that as I was teaching, I sent the angry lady love and light and said a prayer for her to be less angry. He was really amazed, and I feel he had a great learning experience about life. This pleased me very much. We later shared the story with my daughter, who benefitted from it as well.

In our society, we are taught as kids to follow all the rules: go to school then college, get a 9–5 job, get married, have kids, make money, etc. Why aren't our kids taught how to be spiritually enlightened? How do they learn to be happy within, to have peace, joy, and happiness, and how to give love and be grateful? Aren't these things more important than following the rules of our society? My best friend and I were having an in-depth conversation about the high divorce rate in our society and wondering if it is a good idea to encourage marriage to our children or not. What I have found so essential along my spiritual journey is to notice how people marry people to help fill a void or to complete themselves in some way. I was one of those people. I placed so many expectations on my husband and I wanted him to make me happy. How could he have made me happy if I was not happy with me?

If we as a whole can learn how to truly love ourselves, then I believe the divorce rate would be much lower. If two people that are whole and healthy marry, they do not need each other to live and feel good. They can make each other feel better than they already do within themselves. Yes, it is great to be loved and adored as long as you love and adore yourself. The problem with so many marriages is that each person expects the other to make them happy, and this is way too much pressure for anyone to accomplish. Wouldn't it be great to be in love and expect nothing from each other—just enjoy each other and give gratitude and love on an even bigger level? Definitely, both partners must have self-worth and self-love, not just one because it will not work. I will encourage marriage to my children, because I feel that having a family is a wonderful feeling. I will just make sure that I try to instill in my children how important it is to love and cherish themselves to grow into healthy adults and have healthy relationships.

I am so happy and proud of my children, because at such young ages they are already so spiritual. My kids are filled with joy and happiness, yet at the same time, they are very loving and grateful toward themselves and others. I am truly blessed to have the honor of being their mom.

Chapter 14

It Is an Individual Journey

When I started writing this book, I wrote everything by hand in my favorite journal called *Inspiration*. Each page in my journal has a different quote and a word to inspire. I would like to share some of these words and touch on what they mean to me. *Inspire, dream, create, love, imagine, believe, awaken,* and *happiness* are the main words on every page of my journal. Could you imagine if every person in the entire world would strive to live and create these habits in their daily lives? The world would be so enlightened, happy, and peaceful. Each and every one of us is seeking and searching for happiness, and we all have the capability to become happier if we use the proper tools within ourselves. When we are inspired to help ourselves find inner peace and happiness, we inspire others to do the same.

"When you are inspired: dormant
forces, faculties, and talents become

> alive, and you discover yourself to
> be a greater person by far than you
> ever dreamed yourself to be."
> ~Patanjali

When we imagine what we want our lives to be, we are in a dream-like state of being. We are dreaming and creating images of what we inspire to be. One way that I express my dreams and visions is on boards throughout my house. I cut out pictures and quotes and place them on a board to create what I want to manifest in my future. The more creative our imaginations are, the more attainable our dreams become. When we believe something with our entire beings, we can manifest things into reality. The mind is such a powerful tool. We must believe and have faith in whatever we are imaging, dreaming, or creating, and it will come true when the time is right. When you start living from your spirit, you awaken to a new you and become alive from a resting place. Living with love and gratitude brings many new and wonderful people, places, and things into your life.

On my spiritual journey to awaken my soul and live from my spirit, I had to utilize each of these habits to bring myself to a higher level of existence. I have always loved to inspire people throughout my life; now I was becoming inspired to help guide others to learn as well. Recently, not only have I been inspiring others to take care of their bodies, but it was their minds as well. I am teaching others to take control of their lives—spiritually, emotionally, and physically—by waking up to the reality that they need to change their mind-set. People need to stop dwelling on the past and stop worrying so much about every little detail in their lives, be positive, and live for today.

Although I love to teach and inspire others to learn about spiritual enlightenment and finding inner peace, it is up to each and every individual to put in the work to awaken their spirits. Only you can help you; no one else can do it for you. On a daily basis, I meet so many people who are suffering in one way or another, yet they do not want to try to heal. These people want to continue to play the victim card and expect others to feel sorry for them. It is very hard to change old habits of letting go of the past and not stress over the future, but it is possible. Living in the moment and having faith in a higher power are choices that we have the freedom to choose. Everyone who asks me how and why I look so much healthier and happier gets the same answer: let go. I go into depth to those individuals that want to hear more, and they get so intrigued and inspired to change, yet they don't. I can lead the horse to water, but only the horse can drink it. Why is it so hard for people to become disciplined enough to try to help themselves?

When I train my clients, I am only with them thirty to sixty minutes, a couple of times a week. It is what they are doing without me that will make or break their success. I cannot go home with each and every client and make sure that they are following the healthy lifestyle that I taught them. The same thing goes for my acquaintances and friends that love to hear me teach them about mind, body, and spirit-centered ways to live. They need to eat healthily, think positively, and practice meditation in order to live from a more spiritual path.

Everyone wants to be healthier and happier, and everyone wants to find inner peace and be fit and trim. The problem is that most people do not want to put forth the effort it takes to makes these things happen. Why? Why are people so reluctant? For people like me who are driven and go-getters, it is very hard to grasp the concept that it can't be done. We believe that anything and everything can be accomplished with much effort. It is not easy to lose weight and keep it off, and it is not easy to control your thoughts and change your way of thinking. Nothing in life that is worth fighting for comes easily.

When I began my daily practices, it took time to see changes. Behavioral therapists say that it takes approximately ninety days to change a behavior or create a new one. If you stick to your new behavior with discipline, dedication, and consistency, you will succeed. When you begin to see and feel the peace within your soul, the results will shock you. I could not believe how much better I felt when I practiced my meditation and positive mind-set on a daily basis.

There are so many naysayers and people that do not believe they can change or that there is such thing as spiritual enlightenment. These people state, "I am unlucky. I am cursed. My childhood controls and has damaged my life. I cannot let go of the past, no matter how hard I try." And so on. None of this is true. We *all* have the power to let go of the past, be positive, control our thoughts from negative mind clutter, manifest our dreams, and have happy lives. I have felt positive and happy most of my life. What I struggled with was finding inner peace. Although I was happy, I never found that middle ground of a peaceful balance. I was either very happy and excited or down and a little sad. I wasn't so extreme to have any psychological disorders like bipolar disorder, but I could never just be in the middle and be peaceful.

It took me a solid three months of doing all of my homework toward spiritual enlightenment to feel the changes within my soul, that inner peace I was seeking. When I started to find that balance within, everything I had been going through became a little bit easier. My divorce was one of the main events causing me pain, and it became easier to deal with when I could control my thoughts better. As I began to grow and live more from my spirit, I was able to release so many negative thoughts and feelings. I let go of more anger and stopped blaming my ex-husband for things that were not his fault. I had been holding on to so much pain from the past that I was unable to move forward. Once I began to release these thought patterns, my soul was filled with more peace and happiness. I was able to become friends with my ex, and it was so much healthier for both of us. We have been able to peacefully coparent our kids and get along so everyone is happy.

Lisa Dwoskin

Life is so much easier when you live from a place of love and gratitude and not of hate or anger. If you do the work, you will awaken your spirit. Do not choose to live from a dark and dreary place filled with negativity and regret from your past. Live in the moment. Treat every day as a brand-new and exciting chance for you to live life to the fullest. Connect with your true self, the one deep within your soul. We all have a voice, deep within our soul, where our truth resides. We can find it by practicing the different habits and methods discussed in this book. Establishing new habits will take time, but if you listen to the voice within your soul, the truth will reveal itself and you will be guided along your journey toward your destination. My truth and inner voice were showing me signs for four years, and I chose not to listen, because I did not do the work. I was not ready. Sometimes, whether you are ready or not, your inner voice will get so loud that you will have no choice but to listen, and it will not guide you in the wrong direction.

Believe, and you will achieve greatness.

Chapter 15

Be True to You

In order to find or hear the truth within your soul, you must accept and love the real you. Let go of guilt, expectations, perfection, and the opinion of others, and just be you. Being you is accepting the good and the bad, the happy and the sad, at all times. You are enough! You are beautiful in so many different ways, because you are unique. Believe in yourself, be kind to yourself, love yourself, and accept yourself.

When you are feeling, acting, or behaving in ways that are not usual for you, accept it. When it takes time to feel peace and joy in your heart, accept it. If you are bitchy, moody, angry, or irritable, accept it, work through it, and move on. Do not punish yourself or hate yourself for feeling negative or bad feelings; accept it. We are all human and will encounter mood swings and negativity. This is okay. Learn to work through the ups and downs and accept them as they come. Growth is about living and learning and accepting challenges in life. With our spiritual growth, we will have fewer negative encounters and we will know how to handle them. We have learned the tools to help us through the challenges in life come from a spirit-centered mind-set instead of an ego-centered one.

Although I have done my homework and grown so much in the past year, I still encounter challenges in life. My divorce has been extremely challenging for me. I compare Jorge's death and my divorce in so many ways. Divorce feels like a death! Although I know that my path changed and that my marriage was over, it was still sad to end a thirteen-year relationship. Our relationship had many good memories, and we shared a lifetime together. We started a family, a business, a new house—an entire life together. So walking away was challenging. I had many days when I would cry and be sad. In the past, I would get mad at myself, analyze myself, feel guilty, and hate myself. Now, I accept myself and understand that this is part of my grieving period. This is me, and I accept every feeling—good or bad—that I encounter. I listen to my heart, my intuition, my truth, and my spirit, and I know that I will be okay in time. Timing is everything; it is all a process we must go through to get to the next chapter. We all want to feel better right away, but we must allow the process to happen and accept everything that comes our way. Once again, we must let go and surrender in order to heal.

My eight-year-old daughter had a sleep-over with her best friend the other night; she is also eight years old. As I was putting them to bed, they had many questions for me about themselves and the boys in their class. They were revealing their crushes to each other and me for the first time. They were asking me how they would know if their crushes like, or would like, them. They were so concerned and worried that the boys might not like them. My daughter's friend was telling me that she tries to make her hair perfect and smile a lot so her crush will like her. She was extremely worried about it. I thought they were so cute and I needed to set them straight. I told them that all they need to care about is whether or not they like the boys. I said if you are true to yourselves, most boys will like both of you. I reassured them that they are both such beautiful and loving girls, inside and out, and I said boys would be crazy not to like them. Telling them that they need not to worry and just be themselves, I said that the ones that are meant to be will be and the ones that are not for them will not matter. We talked about their kind and loving hearts and spirits, their confidence, their self-worth. I really made them think and accept that they are enough, by just being themselves. I said, "If a boy likes you for being you, that is all that matters, because he will like the true *you*." They loved all of this talk and thanked me so much for listening and explaining things to them. My daughter's friend took a deep breath and said, "Thank you, Lisa, because now I feel so much better about myself and I won't worry as much about the boys."

I loved the fact that they really grasped the concept at such a young age, and enjoyed learning about it as well. It made me think about what society teaches our kids and why they can't learn to just be true to themselves. Imagine how different our lives would be as adults if we truly loved and believed in ourselves from such a young age. I wish that the stores sold magazines about this, instead of those about looks: weight, clothes, hair, makeup, and such superficial things for little girls to worry about at such young ages.

Boys need to share their feelings and love themselves as well. They do not need to be taught to always be strong and tough. They can be human too. As parents, we need to instill in our children the lesson to love themselves exactly as they are. We need to teach them about self-worth, self-acceptance, self-love, and self-esteem by being true to themselves.

I am so grateful to have had parents teach this to me at a young age. My mom taught me so much about self-love and my dad taught me so much about self-worth. Yes society did affect me, as did the bullying in school, but at least I had a foundation. Without a foundation, I could have come out completely different. If I did not have a strong backbone from childhood, maybe I could have been suicidal. Maybe without the self-esteem and self-worth that my parents taught me, I would have become a drug addict. I am grateful to my parents for taking the time to teach me how to love myself. I had many friends growing up that did not get that from their parents, and it showed in them as individuals. My mom was such an angel. She would try to mother all the kids that did not get love from their parents. All my friends feel that my mom was a mother to them, and they all looked up to my dad as being a great father as well. I was truly blessed with a wonderful family. This is so important in your later life.

On the other end of the spectrum, there are many adults that had horrible families and found self-love on their own or from mentors. It is possible to learn self-love at any point of time throughout your life, by being true to yourself and accepting everything about yourself.

Chapter 16

Acceptance of Just Being

The hardest part of my journey has been to understand and accept that I do not have to find or change anything to become more peaceful and spiritual. People are constantly trying to make themselves feel better by filling the empty parts of their lives. I did this too. Like I said, I would exercise to escape my pain or stress. I tried to find happiness in being a mom to my kids, as well as being a wife and a businesswoman, not to mention having a great body and anything else external. What I have come to realize is that none of these things have anything to do with inner peace and joy. Yes, all of these things can make you feel joyful or add happiness to your life, but none of them will awaken your soul to get to a higher state.

When I sold the business, moved out of my house, and left my husband, I wanted to fix my pain and get over all the shifts as soon as possible, so I could start to feel good. The way that I used to deal with all these changes was to replace pain with pleasure. I wanted to place Band-Aids on my pain or get through it as fast as possible. I did not like letting go of anything, and I did not like change. I liked stability and certainty. When I decided to take this journey, I could not do it half-assed. I needed to be all or nothing, and all meant to live in the pain, live in the change, and *be* the change.

At first, I thought I was committed fully toward my walk into spiritual enlightenment, but I was not. When my kids were with their dad, I went out with my friends a lot. Upon going out, I drank many drinks and frequented many bars, clubs, and restaurants, where I met a lot of men. I thought it was fun to be free and let loose, but I would come home at night feeling so empty. I became uninterested in dating altogether, sick of alcohol, and tired of going to bed so late. I would rather hang out with my kids, go to the beach, listen to my friend play the guitar, or go to dinners with some family and have some wine. This was mellower and I enjoyed it, but there was still something missing. I realized that I while I was doing my meditation, reading, writing, and positive affirmations every day, I was still filling my nights and weekends with many busy activities. I was not fully awakening my soul to feel, just partially. I still was trying to predict the future, daydream about future partners, lead my career, think about my past, and dwell on the unknown.

It took months and months and many books for me to realize that it is a process to be on this journey. It does not happen overnight, and you cannot make it happen; it just happens. The more you try to figure out the when, where, and how your journey will take place, the longer it will take. You just need to wake up every day, do the work, and not think, analyze, or worry whether it is working or not. Whether you are growing spiritually or not, you have to open your heart. With an open heart, mind, and spirit, it will work. One day you will wake up and feel the peace a little more than you felt the day prior. What happened to me was the more I would change, the less that I would do, control, or pursue. I noticed that I stopped going out as much, because I was okay with just staying home and reading or watching a good movie. I was okay with just being with myself. I grew very thirsty to educate myself more, and I was reading one or two books a week on spiritual enlightenment and other people's experiences.

Don't get me wrong. I still worked, I was still a mom, and I still pursued my dreams and goals, just with more peace. Before, things would be more stressful and I would have uneasy feelings within. Now I felt this inner peace that was just there. The peace I felt was not small or large; it was just there. I had lost that feeling of being so high or so low. Yes, things would excite me, or things would make me sad, but the extreme levels dissipated. I remember that previously, I would wake up every day with a plan, a mission, deadlines, structure, and expectations and get stressed if I did not complete everything as planned. Now, I was able to get things done and then let the universe guide me. As my spirituality grew, the universe was sending me exactly what I needed in the exact order that was meant to be. All of a sudden, I stopped worrying about things; things just happened.

During the process of spiritual growth, you want it to be fast, and you want to become spiritually enlightened overnight. You want to search and find and conquer this inner peace feeling. This is not how it works at all! There is nothing to find and nothing to conquer. You just have to be in the moment. Every moment that you are awake is a moment *to be*. If you release the fear, the want, and the need and just surrender, you will be. When you are being love, being gratitude, being in spirit, your soul will begin to change. One day you will just realize that you feel the peace within, and when this happens, your journey has just begun. It is a continuous process that will last a lifetime and beyond.

Chapter 17

Simplicity versus Depth

Today I was training a client of mine, and I was sharing with her how the meaning of being in the moment is so simplistic. She is a family counselor and shares the same spiritual beliefs as me, and she elaborated on my comment. She said yes, it is a simplistic term, but it has a very deep meaning to actually live that way. She was sharing with me how so many of her clients do not want to dig deep within their souls and figure out what to release, or how to let go of old patterns. People want to just fix things or fill the void until the pain goes away. Truthfully though, being in the moment and living that way is not so simple, because you must face some deep truths about yourself that most people do not want to face. She and I both agreed that it is so much easier to be alone to work on yourself over a period of time. We both had gone through divorce and decided to take the time to grow and allow ourselves to heal and become whole again, before jumping into another relationship. When you take the time to point the finger toward yourself, you discover many things about yourself that you never realized. When you begin to realize how many expectations and obligations that you placed on yourself and your significant other, you will be shocked.

I am not saying that you should end a good relationship. No. Just take some time to work on yourself from the inside, in or out of a relationship. If you have ended your relationship, do not jump into another one right away. You don't have to be alone forever. Just give yourself some time to heal and grow within yourself. When you are alone and can sit with your pain, you will work through it and release it. Solitude is so important for your spiritual growth that you will feel empowered. Many people cannot ever be alone. How can this be? If people cannot be alone and be happy within themselves, how could they be happy with someone else? The person that is not happy within looks toward another to bring them happiness, and this is why relationships so often come to an end. Who can ever expect another person to make you happy? Relationships should add to your already existing happiness.

I never realized how many people truly do not like themselves until I started writing this book. I always knew that people tend to be hard on themselves, but there are so many that actually do not love themselves at all. Self-love is the most important component toward spiritual growth or enlightenment. In order to gain self-love, you must learn self-acceptance, and this comes from being kind and loving toward yourself.

Another example came from a friend of mine regarding what she was going through in her life. She has a daughter who is my daughter's friend, and she is filled with guilt, hurt, and regret for being a single mom. She regrets not forcing the father to be more involved. She feels guilty that she has to work so hard to provide for her daughter and therefore has less time to be with her. She feels hurt when she gets mad at her daughter for not listening and needs to discipline her. She called me today and cried because the father finally wants to meet his daughter after eight years, and she doesn't know what to do. She also was crying because she is so overwhelmed from everything life has been showing her. I listened to her express herself, and when she was finished, I gave her two minutes of my advice.

In the past when friends would express their issues with me, I listened and tried to give advice on how to fix or change things in their life. I looked at their patterns and pointed out what they needed to do differently. I did this with my clients as well. My psychology degree has always enabled me to effectively listen, dissect, analyze, and give solutions to people's problems. Since I began my spiritual journey, my advice and feedback have changed drastically.

Now what I find myself saying so often is very similar and repetitive toward everyone. Be kind and loving to yourself. Do not feel guilty for anything that has happened in the past. Do not worry or stress so much about the future. Let go, have faith, and believe that God and the universe will guide you in the right direction. Everything that has happened to you in the past and everything that is happening to you now is all for a higher purpose. Accept what has happened and continue moving forward with love and kindness toward yourself. It is amazing how much this impacts people's lives. It makes them sit back and think, *Wow, I am not kind toward myself. I am so hard and critical of myself. I fill myself with unloving thoughts and guilt.* Then when they let go and believe in a higher power to help them, it brings them a sense of peace. All of this is changing the way you think, feel, and act. This is why I say it is so simple to just be. Yes, you need to reach deep inside yourself to grow and change, but once you do, it feels so simple. We all have fears, and we need to dig deep within to gain the strength to let go of the fears that are tying down our spiritual growth.

I listen to so many people complain and stay in frustration with themselves or their significant other, yet they never make the necessary changes or accept that it is their doing, not the other person's. I was so caught up in this cycle as well, and I am not saying it is easy to change, but it is worth trying. So many of us get so angry and frustrated with other people in our lives and let it affect or change our moods. Why do we allow others to affect us when we ourselves have control of our emotions?

If someone else is saying or doing something to upset us, we need to turn it around and accept the fact that we can let it get to us or we can release the anger. If it involves something that we are tied into, we can still control our inner emotions. If your spouse is acting like an idiot, let him. Just because he or she is acting like an idiot, it doesn't mean we need to stop them to feel better. No one and nothing can make us feel worse or better; only we can do that to ourselves. I once had a person in my life that would not stop bothering me. No matter what I did, this person just wanted to irritate me every time I ran into her. I allowed it to affect me for some time. I would get irritated, stressed, and angry and didn't know how to make her stop. After learning and living from a different place in my being, it stopped. Every time this person appeared, I was not even bothered anymore. Not only was I not bothered, I would send her love and light and move on. I figured out that it wasn't her; it was me. I was allowing myself to get bothered, and when I stopped, the bad feelings did as well.

This is what I mean about being simple: a simple change in your thinking and feeling, and your life can change. Yes, you must dig deep within your soul to make the necessary changes in your life to allow inner peace to happen, but it is worth every minute. When you reach a point on your journey to be at peace, you have made the shift. Remember the way others act and treat you is their business. The way you accept and react toward people is your business. Do not allow others to dictate your thoughts or feelings; only you should do this. Let yourself be at peace. Let yourself be kind and loving.

Let yourself be happy, because it is a great place to be.

Chapter 18

Stop Seeking and Begin Living

Do not wait until you lose the weight, get the great job, or find the perfect partner to be happy. Be happy now. Live the life you were meant to live now. The universe and our higher source want us to live in abundance today, not only in the future. Release those fears that keep you in bondage and start living now. Break old patterns and begin new patterns—patterns that make you happy and free. We need to create intentions and manifest what we want out of life today and start making things happen. I felt when I began this journey that I had a gift and I needed to share it with the world. The universe guided me and showed me that I need to speak and hold seminars with groups of men and women and help teach them how to meditate and let their healing begin, so I did just that.

My first seminar was with a group of fifteen women. It was nice, small, and intimate, so we were able to have a group discussion and share thoughts and experiences. I started the seminar with a few of my favorite quotes:

"Love yourself, be kind to yourself, believe in yourself, and you will achieve greatness."

- "Let go and let God."
- "Be in the moment."
- "Be kind to others."
- "Imagine what you want out of life, and make it happen."
- "Find your truth, and release your fears."
- "The power we are seeking is within us."
- "Free yourself from anger, fear, guilt, and bitterness, and forgive."

My favorite one of all is from Wayne Dyer, who said, "What others think of you is none of your business." That is so true and far too many people care too much about what others think. When you are okay with you, it doesn't matter what others think.

Next, I made everyone close their eyes and I played my favorite guided meditation for them to listen to for twelve minutes. Brian Weiss has a CD called *Eliminate the Stress in Your Life*. It is wonderful because it is very simple, easy to listen to, and easy to follow. Some people have never meditated before, and it is easier to be guided. When I stopped the meditation, everyone felt relaxed. I wanted everyone to relax so that they would open their minds and hearts and be able to find their truth. I handed out a questionnaire to fill out and share with the group.

The first question was "What are you passionate about?" I said, "This has to be about you and should not include kids, family, etc." What I have found at my seminars is this is a very hard question for many people. Some people go through their lives asleep and don't even know what they are passionate about. I started by sharing my passions of writing, educating, and teaching people how to live a life that is from their spirit. I shared how I love to help people see things in them that they are not seeing. I love educating others on wellness: exercise, nutrition, and a positive mind-set. Each woman in the group began to share her passions, which allowed others to express themselves. Many women expressed passions that had nothing to do with them but more to do with the world as a whole. I made these individuals dig deeper and listen to their souls. If they couldn't come up with anything, they knew what they needed to work on.

The second question I asked was "What are your fears?" This one we elaborated on for the longest time, because everyone has so many and they need to learn how to let them go. I shared that my biggest fear when I began to live a different life was that I wouldn't gain acceptance from others. Also, I feared being alone, not owning my own gym (which was my identity for so long), and messing up my children's lives if I ended my marriage. I told them I had feared any change, the unknown of my future, giving up control, waiting for pain to pass, and worrying that it wouldn't. As I grew more spiritually, I was able to release these fears and stop worrying so much. It is amazing how much healthier we can become when we stop stressing over the things we cannot control.

One woman shared with us how everyone around her is getting sick with diseases, such as cancer and diabetes. She has become so overwhelmed with stress that she can't stop worrying that she or her loved ones will become sick. This way of thinking will only harm you. I explained to her that if she continues on her path of worrying, she might manifest a disease within herself just from the stress. I advised her to begin meditation and start healing and relaxing her mind. So many of the women complained of not being able to sleep because of so much stress, thoughts, and other mind clutter. This is why everyone needs to meditate.

The third question I asked was "What are five intentions you would like to manifest in your life now?" Intentions are so powerful and really work. A big percentage of the group had never made intentions. If we don't write it down and believe something will happen, it likely will not. You can make your intentions come true, just by believing in them. My intentions when I started my journey were to find peace, joy, and happiness within. I intended to find a healthy love where two individuals are whole and complete and together can do wonderful things to help heal the universe. I set an intention to be a great mother and instill spirituality in my children so they would have peace, love, joy, and happiness. I also set an intention to live in the moment every day of my life. Lastly, I wanted to have infinite amounts of abundance in every aspect of my life. For this question, we went around the room and each woman shared one intention. It was a beautiful experience to hear from these wonderful women. Each one was so interesting and unique.

Our fourth question was "Have you ever just *let go* to allow yourself to *be* in the moment?" This is one of my favorite questions, because for most of my life, I never did this either. I was always going a mile a minute, doing for everyone and trying to accomplish everything. I could never just *be*. I was always trying to be happy and positive for everyone else and would always mask my inner feelings. The day I decided to let go and just *BE* is when my life began. I started to enjoy the moments alone. I also found a happy medium. In the past, I was always up or down, and now I am in the middle. Not only did I change internally, but the universe continued to change everything for me as well. Most people do not live in the moment; they worry about the future and stress over the past. Most women in the class needed to hear this segment because it is difficult for people to grasp the concept of living in the moment.

The last question I asked in each seminar was "If you could live a more spiritually centered life, what would you do differently?" My answer was, "Exactly what I am doing now. Live a life of truth from my soul, live passionately, love myself and others, and just be in the moment." Most of the women in the seminar wanted to meditate more and learn how to become more open. This is a good question, because it makes you think and write down what you need to do to grow spiritually. Thinking and writing about it helps to put the action into motion.

One woman said, "It all sounds so simple, so why do we not do it?" It is simple. Be kind and loving to yourself. I gave them all homework as the seminar ended. I said, "Meditate; say positive affirmations in the morning, afternoon, and evening; do one act of kindness to a stranger every day; and be grateful for every moment that you are living.

I ended with this prayer on being ready to accept the new you:

> Begin to become familiar with the truth in your soul, to be what you are destined to be, to live from your truest and highest state of being, to let go of worry and fear, to live free of worrying about acceptance of others, to intend to become all you are meant to be, to manifest your dreams now, and to honor your life and your soul's purpose. You are magnificent, you are enough, and you are remarkable. From this day forward, be all that you are, and that is when the truth will be revealed to you.
> Namaste.

After the seminar, we took a group photo so I could keep the wonderful memories of my first seminar.

Everyone came up, hugged me, and thanked me, and we all felt lighter and full of love. One woman pulled me aside and wanted to talk privately. Through tears she thanked me and told me that, this night would begin her journey. She expressed that she had been through so much and this was exactly what she needed at this exact moment. I could relate so much to her because I had been in her shoes less than a year before, and it was scary. She thanked me for giving her guidance and the right tools to work with to help her in her life. She also told me that she was so happy to see me grow and become a more spiritual person. She had known me for three years and was a member of my gym. She told me that I looked lighter (in the sense of being less stressed), younger, happier, and more peaceful, and she knew that it could help her as well.

As I drove home by myself, I was so happy. I was happy because I knew without a shadow of doubt that I made a difference in those women's lives that night. The universe guided me through many twists and turns in the last couple of years, and it landed me exactly where I am meant to be. I am a guide, teacher, and educator, and when I do this and help others, it brings joy, peace, and happiness to my heart and soul. I am so blessed to be on the journey, and I am so thankful to all of the teachers that I had along the way. I know that I will continue to grow spiritually, and I will continue to talk to groups of people in the future. I was destined for greatness, and I have found my path.

Namaste.

Chapter 19

Note to Self

Dear Lisa:

I am your spirit, your truth, your guide. I want you to listen to me, believe in me, and follow my guide. You are a wonderful, beautiful, kind, loving, and compassionate soul. You are enough! You were put on this earth to help teach and guide others to live their lives as if they are in heaven, filled with an abundance of love and gratitude. Teach others that they do not have to wait until they die to experience peace. Peace is something that we are meant to have every day in our lives. Open your heart and your soul toward spiritual enlightenment. Do your homework and silence your mind through meditation on a daily basis; it will help you. When you quiet your mind, you will hear your inner voice that resides in your spirit; listen to it. You have nothing to find. You must *be*. Be in the moment. Be true to yourself every moment of every day. Let your spirit guide you along your journey or path of life. Stay on course, filled with love and gratitude, and the truth with find you. There will be challenges along the way, and it will be okay. You will take many twist and turns until you have reached your destination. Once you have reached your destination, you will learn and grow some more, because the teachings are never ending. Each and every experience that you encounter will help you find your way toward spiritual enlightenment. It will not be an easy road, but only you must make this journey for yourself.

I will place many tools in front of you, and it will be up to you to use them. I will guide you and show you the way, but you must do the work. There will be people that I place in your life. Some will stay, and some will go; trust in me. Open your heart and let go of the people that have served their purpose in your life.

Wake up each and every morning and tell yourself that you are enough, you are love, and you are truth. Be kind and accepting of who you are. Read your daily affirmations and fill your mind with positive thoughts. When the negative thoughts creep in, feel them, work through them, and release them. Heal yourself by living in the moment. Release the pain of the past. Do not worry about the future, and be in the moment; live for today. Be love, gratitude, joy, passion, happiness, and peace. You will find your truth and you will become a teacher to help others find their way toward a spiritually enlightened life. Believe, and you will achieve greatness along this wonderful journey called life.

Namaste.

The Universe

Favorite quote from *Eat, Pray, Love*

"If you are brave enough to leave behind
everything familiar and comforting
and set on a truth-seeking journey
either externally or internally. If you
are truly willing to regard everything
that happens to you on that journey as
a clue. If you accept everyone you meet
along the way as a teacher. If you are
prepared to face and forgive some very
difficult realities about yourself, then the
truth will not be withheld from you."
~Elizabeth Gilbert

Seminar Questions and Answers

When I started to give my seminars, there were so many of the same kinds of questions asked by the different people. Most of my seminars were filled with women, with a few men in attendance. We always started off with a meditation; this would open up everyone's heart and put us all in a place of relaxation. Meditation lasted about ten to twenty minutes. Once this was finished, we introduced ourselves. If it was a small group, I asked everyone to share what they wanted to get out of the seminar. If it was a large group, I took questions to help me teach what I had learned. I would like to go over some of these questions and comments and shed some light as to what I learned and shared during these seminars.

How do you teach yourself to be happy?

You don't. You teach yourself to love yourself, be kind to yourself, and your happiness will come through this. You share love to yourself and others. You let go of negativity and live from a positive place filled with love and gratitude. Open your heart to the unknown and fill every moment with belief and faith. Let go, and just *be*.

Aren't I being selfish if I just start to love myself more than I love my family or friends?

No. You must love yourself before you can truly give love to anyone or anything. You must establish self-worth, self-love, and self-acceptance. If you continue to give to others more than yourself, you will lose your sense of self. Yes, it is great to give love to others, as long as you are giving it to yourself first. So many people in my seminars say that when they help others, they feel better about themselves because they are making a difference in someone's life. Yes, it is great to help others; the problem is many of us help others because we do not want to look at ourselves and face the fact that we are not okay. Many women give to their husbands, children, coworkers, and friends, and they neglect themselves. This is not good. Be kind and loving to yourself first.

I have too many obligations with work and providing for my family. How will I ever find the time for spiritual development?

Do you find time to go out to dinner? Everyone has the time. All it takes is a little bit of effort: ten minutes a day to meditate, two minutes to look at yourself in the mirror and say positive things, five minutes of reading positive affirmations, and the rest of the day you stay in a loving state. When life takes a turn and you run into something negative, turn it around as best as you can. Self-talk, self-love, and self-acceptance do not take time out of your day. Be patient, kind, and loving toward yourself every day, and that will be enough.

I am stuck! I cannot quit my job, leave my spouse, or change my life right now. My life will never get better.

It is not about your job, spouse, or life. It is about you. I left all of these things behind, and it did not change me. *I* changed me. It was actually harder making the change among all of these shifts occurring in my life. Change happens internally, not externally. Remember it is a process that takes place within your soul over time. Do the homework that I have talked about and you will see your life shift. You will begin to feel that inner peace just from making the changes within yourself.

I get so angry and upset when I try to share my spiritual journey with my family or friends and they begin to criticize or tell me it's nonsense.

It is none of your business what others think of you. All that you should be concerned with is how you feel. Share with others if you want, but accept their resistance and do not let it affect you. Do not try to convince anyone to take your journey or path; just continue on. People in your life will notice a difference in you, and once they do, they will be more open to listen. Stay on course.

How can you just be, when there is so much negativity surrounding you?

Then be in the negativity. Feel all the negative thoughts with kindness toward yourself. Allow yourself to feel all the bad. Don't fight it or feel guilty. Just be in it. Eventually, by being kind and loving toward yourself, and allowing yourself to be in it, it will pass. When it passes, you would have allowed yourself to work through it and not deny it or push it away—or place a Band-Aid over it. People who lose loved ones to death or divorce need to grieve. Those who do not grieve and meet someone new or hide from their feelings always pay the price in the future. Do not try to feel happy when you are not. Just try to love and be kind to yourself at all times, good or bad.

I have come so far along my journey and I feel the change. My husband makes me so mad because he has not followed the path and he remains the same.

Do not try to change anyone else but yourself; this will not work. Once your spouse sees changes in you, the dynamic of the relationship will change. The other person will usually benefit from your changes because they will feel less stress. There will be fewer demands, fewer expectations, less anger, less fear, etc. In time, they will either join you on the path or you will go on different paths. Either way, it will be okay, because the universe will guide you and show you what is right for you and your higher self. Sometimes, this will mean that you let go and move on without fear. I had to let go after holding on so tightly and for so long, but it is okay now. My soul needed to move on.

I have done the homework and stayed on path, and I do not feel or see a difference in my life.

Be patient, loving, and kind toward yourself, and it will happen. You are trying too hard, and you are expecting an outcome. This is not the way to grow spiritually. Let go of all expectations and surrender, and it will happen when the time is right. One day you will just feel differently; trust me. Continue to move forward in a way of love and gratitude. Continue to open your heart, silence your mind, and meditate.

Why have so many negative and horrible things happened to me in my life? It is not fair! My childhood was so bad and painful, and I did not deserve it! How could anyone get past so much tragedy?

You must let go of the past. Forgive. Send love and light toward whatever happened, and let it go. This will be a process; it will not be easy, but it must be done. Holding onto the anger and the regret from the past will only hurt you now and in your future. Everything that has happened to you was meant to be, to bring you toward a higher understanding of God, faith, and the universe. Feel the pain, live it all over again, but this time, let go of anger, guilt, and fear and accept yourself with love, peace, and kindness. Let it go, once and for all. Do not allow yourself to be a victim for one more minute; allow yourself to be free of the pain. You are enough! You deserve a life filled with abundance, joy, and love. Believe in yourself, love yourself, and you will be okay.

No matter how hard I work, I can never make enough money to support my family. It is a never-ending battle, day in and day out.

Stop fighting and worrying about the lack of money. The more you dwell on what you do not have, the more this will show up in your life. Be thankful and grateful for what you do have. You have a job. You have a house, food, and money to live. Let go of the worrying and fill yourself with the love, and be grateful for every day, every moment, and everything that you do have, and you will attract more of this. Continue moving forward with your practice, and it will happen for you.

What is my purpose in life? I am so lost and cannot see clearly.

If you do not know what your soul's purpose is, do not try to find it, because you will not. Again, do your homework and become more spiritually enlightened.

Open your heart and your soul to grow toward the light, love, and gratitude of life. Let go of all control; be kind and loving toward yourself. The more you can just *be* in the moment, the more that the universe will show you, when you are ready. Do not try to search for it, get it, or find it. Just be still. When you quiet your mind with meditation, things will be shown to you. You might have dreams. People will start to show up in your life to guide you. You must believe in a higher power to guide you by surrendering all control.

I have noticed that some of my friends have disappeared from my life along my journey. Why?

People are brought into your life to serve your soul's higher purpose. When you have learned all there is to learn from someone, they and you will move on. It is okay to let go of people once they have served their purpose in your life and once you have served your purpose in theirs. Sometimes, the people will come back in the future and teach you more, or you will have learned from them. It is okay to trust that the universe will place the right people in your life at the exact right moment. This has always happened to me, and I love it.

Why do some people get so freaked out when you mention spirituality, as if they think it is some sort of a religion?

Yes, I have heard this often. People are filled with fear of the unknown. Some people do not like organized religion or believe in God. Spirituality is not about God or religion. It is about love and truth, and living from a higher purpose. I believe in and pray to God, but I also ask the universe to guide me. You can choose to believe in whatever higher power you want; it could be any kind of energy source that you choose. It is important to believe that something is helping to guide us on our path, wherever it might be. Spirituality is not some sort of hocus–pocus or magic; it is pure and honest love.

Author Biography

Lisa Dwoskin has a degree in both Psychology and Exercise Physiology from the University of Miami. She has owned and operated Metamorphecise Spa and Health Club in Pembroke Pines, Fla. for the past 13 years. She is a life coach, personal trainer,  and group exercise instructor. As Lisa became more experienced in working with clients one on one, she realized that many people were suffering and staying stagnant in one place due to the fact that they could not program their minds to be positive. Lisa felt that she had to teach individuals that with a positive mind, they can change their bodies and their lives. This is when she incorporated mind and spiritual workouts into her clients regimens.

Lisa has been in the health and wellness industry for about 25 years, since she was 18 years old. She built up a great reputation for herself and people want to hear what she has to say. She leads seminars twice a month to educate people on self-love, healing, and meditation. She talks about fitness, nutrition, spiritual enlightenment, and healthy living. She not only teaches what she preaches, but she lives it as well 100 %.

Lisa lives, breathes, eats and sleeps fitness! Anyone that knows Lisa is drawn to her by her positive, magnetic personality and her knowledge and love for fitness, and well being. "Life is a gift and you must give back to truly enjoy it!" Lisa lives her life to help people, she believes that your mind is in control of your body, train your mind to be strong and positive is her motto: "If you believe, you will achieve greatness!